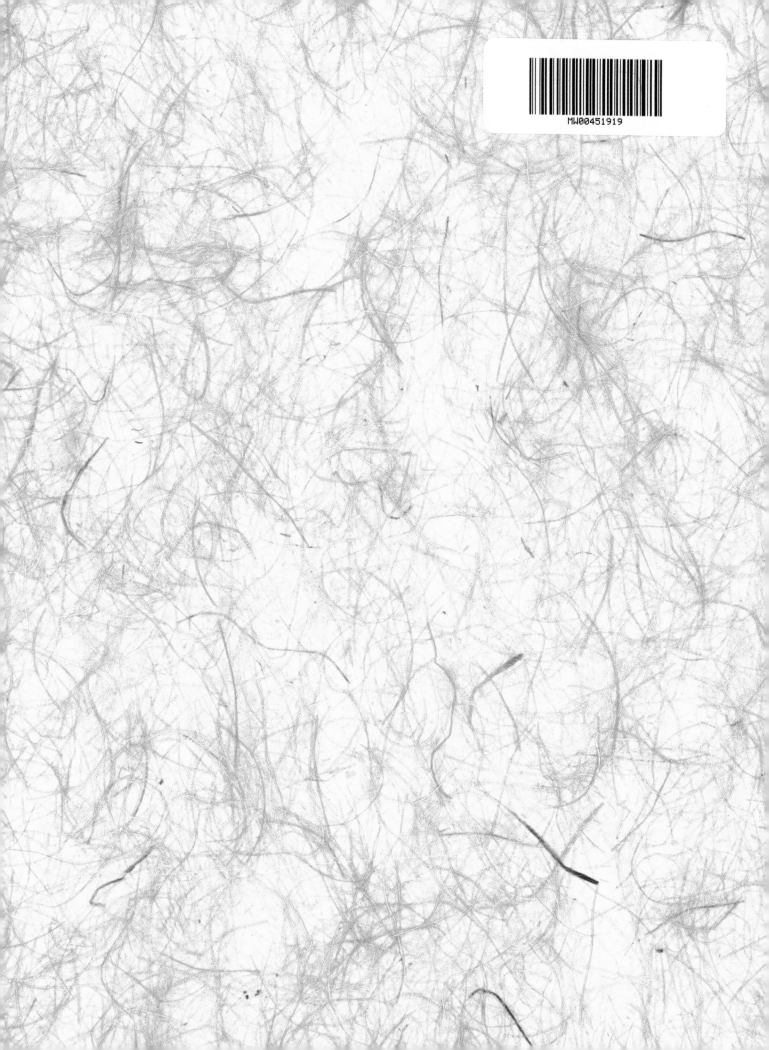

MW00451919

WOOD ART TODAY
Furniture, Vessels, Sculpture

Dona Z. Meilach

4880 Lower Valley Road, Atglen, PA 19310 USA

Dedicated to my parents, Rose and Julius Zweigoron,
for being raised in a hardware store where tools were my toys.

*"Technology has been a miracle for people with creative and prolific ideas.
They can do more in their lifetime."* Po Shun Leong

"For me, making art cannot be separated from living." Meredith Sattler

Other Books by Dona Z. Meilach
Architectural Ironwork
Art Jewelry Today
Box Art
Contemporary Art with Wood
Contemporary Blacksmith
Contemporary Stone Sculpture
Creating Modern Furniture
Decorative & Sculptural Ironwork
Direct Metal Sculpture
Small Wood Objects as Functional Sculpture
Woodworking, The New Wave
And others

Library of Congress Cataloging-in-Publication Data

Meilach, Dona Z.
    Wood art today : furniture, vessels, sculpture / by Dona Z.
Meilach.
        p. cm.
    ISBN 0-7643-1912-4 (hardcover)
1. Woodwork--United States--History--20th century.
2. Turning--United States--History--20th century. I. Title.
NK9610.M45 2003
745.51--dc21
              2003007379

Copyright © 2004 by Dona Z. Meilach

Designed by Dona Z. Meilach
Page layout by Ellen J. (Sue) Taltoan
Type set in Windsor BT/Korinna BT

ISBN: 0-7643-1912-4
Printed in China

Published by Schiffer Publishing Ltd.
4880 Lower Valley Road
Atglen, PA 19310
Phone: (610) 593-1777; Fax: (610) 593-2002
E-mail: Schifferbk@aol.com
Please visit our web site catalog at
www.schifferbooks.com
We are always looking for people to write books on
new and related subjects. If you have an idea for a
book, please contact us at the above address.

This book may be purchased from the publisher.
Include $3.95 for shipping. Please try your bookstore
first.
You may write for a free catalog.

In Europe, Schiffer books are distributed by
Bushwood Books
6 Marksbury Ave. Kew Gardens
Surrey TW9 4JF England
Phone: 44 (0)20 8392-8585; Fax: 44 (0)20 8392-9876
E-mail: Bushwd@aol.com
Free postage in the UK. Europe: air mail at cost.
Please try your bookstore first.

ACKNOWLEDGMENTS

A book that encompasses so much material requires the help and cooperation of many creative, talented people. Primarily, I want to acknowledge each and every artist who submitted photos, brought pieces to me to be photographed, and suggested other artists to contact. Their names accompany their photos in the following pages. My deepest apologies to those whose work was omitted for lack of space. Each chapter could accommodate only so many examples of a particular category and many wonderful photos had to fall on the cutting room floor.

I am grateful to the artists who gladly, anxiously, answered my request to help curate the photos that appear. Frank E. Cummings III, Michael Ireland, and Terry Martin spent hours viewing sheets of transparencies, prints, digital images, and projected slides until they were bleary-eyed and excited about the work they saw.

Jan Peters, David Peters, and Kirsten Muenster of the del Mano Gallery, Los Angeles, California, earn gold stars for their superb cooperation. They provided names of artists they represent, and photos of several pieces from their recent exhibitions.

Other galleries that responded to my requests are Northwest Gallery of Fine Woodworking, Seattle, Washington; William Zimmer Gallery, Mendocino, California; Leo Kaplan Modern, New York, New York; Patina Gallery, Santa Fe, New Mexico; and many others throughout the country.

I appreciate the help received from Albert LeCoff, Executive Director, Wood Turning Center, Philadelphia, Pennsylvania, and Terry Martin, Editor of the Wood Turning Center publication, *Turning Points*.

Robyn Horn, David Holzapfel, Frank E. Cummings III, and Seymour Zweigoron read portions of the manuscript and provided valuable suggestions.

My sincerest thanks to Sue Kaye, who was always ready to help when I needed her. My thanks, too, to Tom Loeser, Associate Professor of Art, University of Wisconsin, Madison, Wisconsin, who helped alert furniture makers to my needs. And to Edward S. Cooke Jr., Chair of the Department of the History of Art, Yale University, New Haven, Connecticut, for his cogent comments. I wish to acknowledge the wonderful pictures by many photographers whose art form helps to make this such a beautiful book.

My appreciation to Nancy and Peter Schiffer for their willingness to publish modern craft books. As always, I am grateful to my supportive husband, Mel, who constantly reminds me to stand up straight after sitting hundreds of untallied hours at the computer.
Dona Z. Meilach
Carlsbad, California

Please note: Anyone who wishes to contact a specific artist may send a request to the author in care of Schiffer Publishing. Email: Schifferbk@aol.com
In Europe: Bushwd@aol.com

Preface

How does an idea germinate into a book like this?

This book's roots were sown, firmly planted, and grown in the late 1970s and early 1980s when Crown Publishing published five of my books dealing with wood sculpture, furniture, boxes, and small wood objects. After blossoming for many years the books were dormant, but not forgotten. Readers who told me how one book or another had ignited their woodworking careers wrote, phoned, and emailed, asking if I had another wood book in the offing.

Even a quarter century later, artists tell me these "classic" books are on their shelves and often referred to for ideas. They are selling briskly in used book listings. I brought them to the attention of Schiffer Publishing who suggested I write a new book rather than revise the old. Revisiting the subject and the artists has been an exciting venture.

Today, it's easier to gather photos, ideas, and interviews than it was twenty to thirty years ago, thanks to the Internet and the World Wide Web. Within a few months of announcing my needs, I had heard from people whose work appeared in my earlier books, and from many new craftspeople eager and appreciative for the exposure. As photos arrived, they had to be logged in, acknowledged, judged for photo quality and artistic merit.

Within eight months, about 3600 photos were submitted from more than 250 artists in 9 countries. Next was the job of sorting, organizing, and bringing in curators to help select the approximately 500 photos you will see from over 130 artists. Planning the book, designing the pages, writing copy, and sending it to readers to check for accuracy is always a lengthy, time consuming endeavor. At the same time, captions with missing information had to be sent to artists for fleshing out.

When my job of creativity was accomplished, the manuscript was sent to the publisher where the capable staff took over and added graphic elements, designed a cover, and prepared it for printing. As part of that process, proofs had to be read, color galleys checked for photo and copy placement, an index prepared, along with the myriad details involved for bringing a book from manuscript to final form. And thus a new book has taken root, been nurtured, and burst into bloom, ready for the light of day, discovery, and appreciation.

As you peruse these pages, think of it as a major creative project, much like envisioning an idea in a piece of wood, gathering the material, shaping it, sanding it, finishing it, and having viewers enjoy it for a long time.

Opposite page:
Tommy Simpson. **Mittened on You**. *Courtesy artist.*

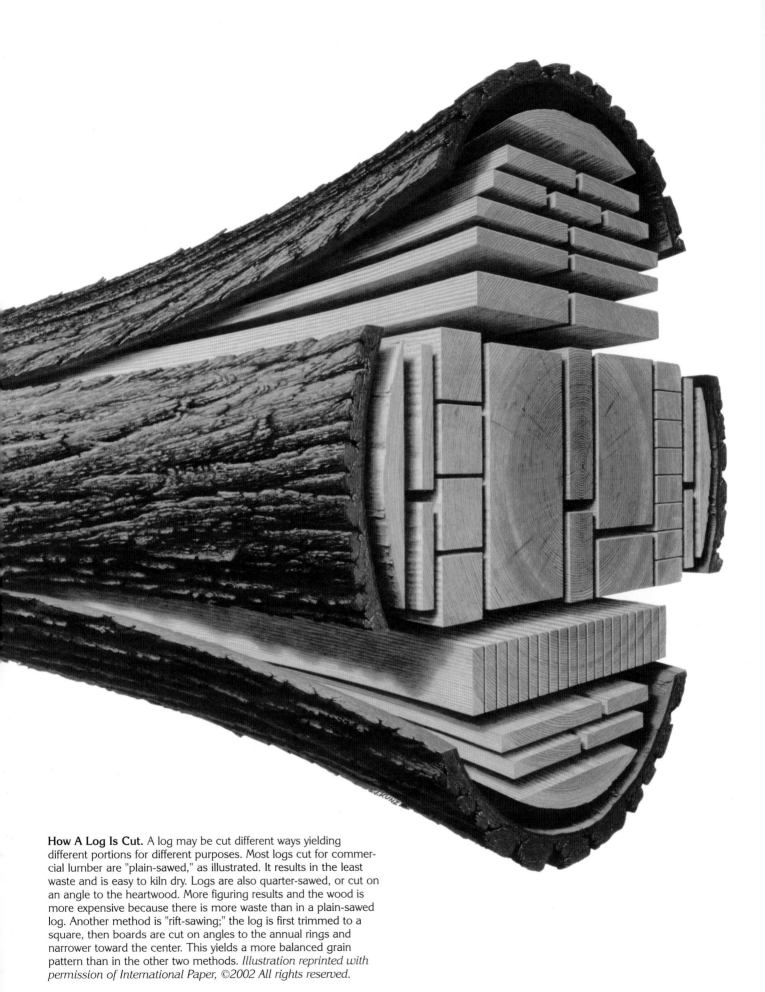

How A Log Is Cut. A log may be cut different ways yielding different portions for different purposes. Most logs cut for commercial lumber are "plain-sawed," as illustrated. It results in the least waste and is easy to kiln dry. Logs are also quarter-sawed, or cut on an angle to the heartwood. More figuring results and the wood is more expensive because there is more waste than in a plain-sawed log. Another method is "rift-sawing;" the log is first trimmed to a square, then boards are cut on angles to the annual rings and narrower toward the center. This yields a more balanced grain pattern than in the other two methods. *Illustration reprinted with permission of International Paper, ©2002 All rights reserved.*

Contents

Acknowledgments 3

Preface 5

Chapter 1- WHY WOOD? 9
    THE TREE 10
    CURING A LOG 12
    FINDING THE SOURCES 14
    TOOLS OF THE TRADE 16
    CLAMPS 18
    WOOD GLUES 18
    COLORANTS 18
    SAFETY 19

Chapter 2- FURNITURE 20
    TABLES 22
    SEATING 44
    DESKS 70
    CABINETS 84
    CLOCKS AND MORE 108
    MIRRORS AND VANITIES 120

Chapter 3- VESSELS, BOWLS, TURNINGS 126

Chapter 4- SCULPTURE-THE WOOD SPEAKS 185

Chapter 5-SCULPTURAL OBJECTS 238

APPENDIX
    Bibliography 254
    Resources 254
    Index 255

Gregg Lipton. **Custom Keystone Sideboard**. Quilted maple, ebony, and frosted glass. Furniture is designed as an accent piece in a foyer or small dining room. 32" high, 50" wide, 20" deep. *Photo, Stretch Tuemmler*

Leon Lacoursiere. **Keeper**. Curly maple and paint. After turning the basic bowl form, he uses his carving skills to penetrate the shape, then paints the edges for contrast. 5.25" high, 6" diam. *del Mano Gallery, Los Angeles, California. Photo, David Peters*

David Groth. **Rooster 2**. Myrtle wood. A sculpture carved using a chain saw and finishing tools. 23.5" high, 29" wide, 9" deep. *Photo, artist*

Chapter 1

Why Wood?

I think that I shall never see
A poem lovely as a tree.
Poems are made by fools like me,
But only God can make a tree.
Joyce Kilmer, Trees

Pick up a twig and toss it for your puppy to retrieve. Look at a tree and admire its beauty, its leaves, and its shape against the sky. Walk in the forest and observe tree trunks and stumps. Trees in their natural state have an untamed beauty. The wood artist tames it.

Trees are plentiful so that their wood is near at hand, versatile, and easily worked with a variety of tools. Man has been taming the beauty of wood, using it for functional and handsome objects almost from the dawn of civilization, and in every culture. That has not changed. Religious idols from early civilizations are precursors of those used today. Boats fashioned from logs, bowls for mixing grains, pipes for smoking, toys for children, musical instruments, and, of course, furniture. Where would humans be without these items? Where would we be without the material from which they are made, without the tools needed, and without skilled, creative artisans, and artists? Even in the most basic societies where furniture is not essential, wood is used to fashion hunting and foraging tools, tent posts, canoes, and myriad other functional items.

Through the years, the use of wood designs have changed with the styles, but many aspects of its use have changed little. Furniture designs from early cultures have been supplanted by newer fashions in different eras. Compare baroque furnishings, for example, with Art Nouveau styles. Compare Victorian furniture with modern. Many older styles are still treasured and emulated. Eventually, today's styles will be supplanted by newer styles. There has always been change; there always will be.

Change is the reason you will find three approaches to wood art in this one book. Most books may deal only with furniture, only turnings, or only sculpture. Today's artists combine these approaches brilliantly and shamelessly. They bypass purism and conventionality as they create. The turner has become a sculptor and may also make furniture. The furniture maker may turn wood for legs, and details, and sculpt portions of furniture that are already three-dimensional items. The sculptor may use all the techniques. No longer is there a great divide between the artists. They are all versatile and, seemingly, never run out of ideas. Optimistically, our forests will never run out of wood.

The examples shown throughout this book are as varied as the people who created them. As different as each object is, they have a commonality. The artists have a knowledge of wood and the tools required to work it. Their usage is a never-ending series of fascinating learning experiences.

A majority of artists have learned to work with the medium and the tools by taking classes, attending workshops, reading books and magazines, and joining woodworking groups for an exchange of ideas. Some have learned their art genetically, so to speak. They have been fortunate to have been raised by parents who were wood workers and who passed on their knowledge. Others are completely self-taught. They have discovered that working with wood is a continuing study, a foray into nature and its myriad vicissitudes.

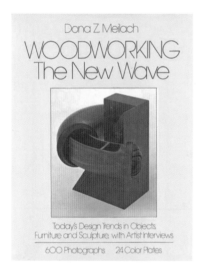

Books by Dona Z. Meilach, published between 1975 and 1985, were an acknowledged catalyst for woodworking careers by several artists. Many have work in this book. The books also provide a historical resource for comparing style trends, and how they have changed over the past quarter century.

The Tree

Trees are complex living entities, brilliant creations of nature. The artist who works in wood must learn several fundamentals of the medium. Most trees fall into a category of either softwoods or hardwoods. Each tree is composed of layers:

1. There is the outer bark layer, composed of a corky dead portion that varies in thickness and texture depending on the species and age of the tree.
2. Next is a thin, inner living bark consisting of the "xylem" and "phloem" that serve as a pipeline through which food is passed. Xylem carries nutrients from the leaves and roots to the tree. Phloem carries dissolved nutrients down to where they are needed.
3. A cambium cell layer is the growing part of the trunk that produces new bark and new wood annually. This is the layer where one can see growth rings and determine a trees age from a cut log.
4. Sapwood is next to the cambium and transports water to the leaves.
5. The heartwood is the central supporting inner section of the tree. It consists of inactive cells that have been slightly changed chemically and physically from the cells of the inner sapwood ring. Heartwood varies in color and texture in various species.

Softwood is easily sawed, carved, and nailed. Examples of softwood trees are pine, fir, spruce, cedar, and hemlock. Most are conifers, (cone bearing trees).

Hardwoods, from which most furniture and the majority of wood turnings are made have different densities that affect their working ability; the harder the wood, the harder it is to use some hand tools. Hardwoods include the familiar woods such as oak, maple, walnut, chestnut, pecan, cherry, and hickory. Mahogany, considered, a hardwood, may vary from hard to soft as far as workability is concerned.

Scientific wood collections exist that have as many as 55,000 samples representing about 12,000 genera and over 20,000 species, mostly of hardwood. In addition to the inherent characteristics of a log, the appearance of a finished object is also affected by the manner in which the log is cut. Cutting a log with the grain direction, across the grain, along the edge, through the heartwood, and on other angles, affects the grain, texture, figure, and color of the wood. It's important to clarify to the differences in the terms.

Grain refers to the direction of the tree's rays or other longitudinal growth elements. *Grain* may be straight, spiral, interlocked, wavy, curly, or irregular.

Texture refers to the relevant variation in the sizes of the cells ranging from fine to coarse, and sometimes uneven. A fine textured wood, such as maple, has small diameter cells. Oak is coarse textured with large diameter cells. Even-textured woods have uniform textured cells. Uneven textured woods show variations of cell diameters.

Figure in a grain pattern is determined by the way the tree grows during different seasons, the part of the tree from which the wood is taken, and how the wood

Andrew Vallee and Wesley Smith. **The Tree Project.** A dramatic representation of how a tree is used was exhibited at the Whatcom Museum of History and Art, Bellingham, Washington, in 2002. A two-inch slab of wood was cut from the length of a tall tree trunk, made into ten benches that were lined up to appear as the tree trunk along the center of the museum's main gallery. It suggested that the tree had stood, and then fallen into furniture. The viewer could walk around the tree, experiencing what it once was and what it had become. Thirty other pieces of furniture on exhibit were crafted from the same tree. *Courtesy, the Whatcom Museum of History and Art. Photo, Gunther José Frank*

was sawed. Oak, walnut, zebrawood, and rosewood are highly grained and figured because they have a rapid summer growth period. Mahogany grows at a more uniform rate so the pattern is more regular. Ebony usually has only grain and no figure.

Unusual appearances in wood, such as speckling, mottling, circling, swirling, quilting, blistering, and so forth, appear where the tree has grown in crotches or V-like areas, or where the trunk separates into branches.

Burls, highly prized by wood turners, are wart-like, usually domed outgrowths from the trunk resulting from a virus that may enter through any break in the bark. They are a benign, but rapid growth of wood cells, much like a wart or a tumor on a human. They are highly figured and the irregular and erratic grain is caused by fibers that expand, compress, and encircle an area as the area grows. Thin slices of burl wood are often used for unusual veneers.

Knots, caused by dead branches are often found within a tree's trunk between and within the rings. The artist may use all these variants advantageously, though sometimes they appear unexpectedly and may interfere with a planned design.

Two other aspects of grain are important to the wood worker; end grain and face grain. End grain is the result of a horizontal cut across a log. Portions of the log's rings, heartwood, and sapwood appear. Face grain runs the length of the cut and dressed board and can produce unique patterns.

Color is usually limited to the tree's heartwood and is the result of compounds in the cell walls and cavities. Considering the thousands of different tree species, and the unique individuality of a tree's growth, color ranges in wood are infinite and may be from the almost white of holly to the jet black of ebony and the chameleon-like characteristics of purpleheart. Wood may also change color when exposed to light for long periods: lighter woods darken and darker woods become lighter.

Spalting. One more aspect of the tree is of vital interest to artistic woodworkers and you will see examples in the objects they create. Spalted woods are the result of some of nature's capriciousness. Spalting is formed by unseen organisms at a specific time and place no one can determine. It is selective in its territory and marks its boundaries with lines of demarcation that hold mystery as well as beauty. Spalted wood is consistently inconsistent in appearance, which makes it in high demand within the decorative wood markets. Each piece is unique and completely different from the next. The lines of spalted wood are intricate and fascinating. With a little imagination, one might see ancient calligraphic symbols, world maps, animals, birds, fish, and mountains. Like clouds, the images may seem to change each time you contemplate what is there. Spalting occurs in many species and, most commonly, in birches, beeches, and maples. But spalting poses problems; if the organisms have been at work too long, the piece of wood may decay.

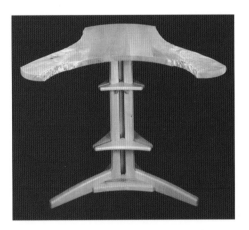

Andrew Vallee and Wesley Smith. **Bar Stool**. Big leaf maple. This stool is one of one of thirty pieces of furniture by Vallee and Wesley, made from the one 118-year-old tree for their Tree Project. *Photo, Gunther José Frank*

David Sengel. **2nd Enro, Ojime, Netsuke**. Banksia seedpod, palm nut, and stone show that even the smallest part of a tree can be used for art. This Japanese netsuke is only 2" high, 8" wide. The Enro vessel is from the banksia seedpod, the fish netsuke is carved of palm nut, and the ojime is a turned stone. *Courtesy, artist*

Curing A Log

A tree retains water in its cells even after it is cut. This water content affects the weight, size, shape, hardness, strength, and stiffness of a log as well as its vulnerability to rot and deterioration from fungi and insects. The water content also determines the changes in these characteristics that will occur when the wood is transported to another environment. The manner in which the wood is dried also affects its usability.

Drying and curing wood properly is essential to minimize quick shrinking that can cause "checks" which are cracks in the wood. Logs must be carefully seasoned to eliminate moisture after they are cut. Lumber companies use various production methods for this process. Logs may be immersed in water until they are ready for the sawmill, and then sawn into boards. Drying may be accomplished by placing stacked boards outdoors in the air, by kiln drying, and by radio-frequency dielectric procedures.

Tree trunks in New Guinea used to support their structures, are carved with ritualistic and symbolic art images. *Photo, Dona Meilach*

12

Wood workers who harvest their own wood have to address the drying procedures, often cutting a log or hoisting a burl and letting it dry outdoors over a period of several months. Some artists like to use green wood because it is easier to work than seasoned wood, but green wood carries an unknown characteristic. What happens as it dries? Will it crack or shrink? It depends on the moisture content and the thickness of the wood. Gary Stevens harvests redwood logs from his property, turns them while green into vessels until they are in a near finished form and about 2-inches thick, Then he puts them in a drying room for two to three months. He knows the characteristics of the redwood that he works with most often and can tell from its weight, and by experience, when it is dry enough. Only then does he finish the vessel. For air-drying lumber, the rule of thumb is one year per inch of thickness.

Working green wood is often preferred for bowl turnings and sculpture because nature's changes may enhance the shape. Conversely, it could create a disaster.

A hollowed tree trunk will be used for a boat. *Photo, Dona Meilach*

Gary Stevens. Stevens harvests old tree stumps and rare pieces of burl redwood that he finds on his property in the Santa Cruz Mountains of California. This burl weighs about 2 tons. From burl or stump to finished sculpture is a long process that may require 6 to 8 months. After cutting, the log has to be stripped of its bark, sawn, shaped, cured, and finished. *Courtesy, artist*

Finding The Sources

Logs can be acquired from a variety of sources such as farms, tree surgeons, city dumps, lumber mills, and from trees on your own property if they exist. If trees are being trimmed in your neighborhood, you may be able to spirit a few cut portions of a trunk to your workshop. The problem with found wood is that it may have foreign objects in it such as nails and hooks. It may be hard to identify unless you know something about trees. Large pieces of log are heavy and there's no point hauling home something that you can't use for anything other than firewood. You can buy that already cut and bundled for carrying.

As mentioned earlier, the study of woods can be an absorbing exploration. Several books listed in the bibliography offer sources for seeking information and suggestions for identifying different woods. Every wood has inherent characteristics such as its primary color, secondary color, pattern of growth rings, pores, grain, hardness, weight, odor, bark, shape of the leaves, and size.

Milled boards are available from lumberyards. Specialty wood suppliers offer exotic species from throughout the world. Sometimes, it's difficult to learn about unfamiliar woods. A search by the name of the wood on an Internet search engine generally turns up a source for that particular wood and many more.

When larger pieces of lumber are required, exotic wood dealers usually have them or can order them, or you may have to laminate pieces together using glues and clamps. A consideration with laminations is that the glues, over time, can dry out. Shrinkage between the glued pieces can be different and create a separation at the glued line.

Recycling used wood is also a viable source for new objects. Woodworkers seek used furniture, old wood from houses, hotels, and public buildings that have been wrecked. The wood is well cured and has endured over time. Fine wood from stair posts, fireplaces, or decorative woodwork in old houses can be recycled advantageously and brilliantly.

No matter what the source of wood or lumber, today's wood artists respect the ecology of the world and try to not waste any of the resources the tree supplies.

William V. Chappelow stands amid his store of different woods from which he makes exotic functional, and collectible utensils, sculpture, and jewelry. Trees that have been cut and dressed into boards become the preferred wood source for many artists.
Photo, Gerry Soifer

To that end, Andrew Vallee and Wesley Smith mounted an exhibition at the Whatcom Museum of History and Art in Bellingham, Washington, in 2002. Their three-year project was designed to raise awareness about the economics of sustainable forestry. Their goal is to show there is an economically viable alternative to clear cutting forests. They are striving to bring issues of forestry to a human level by focusing on the life and transformation of one tree. The tree used for their project combined local and natural history, ecology, environmental art, photography, and furniture making potential.

A big leaf maple tree chosen by Vallee and Smith had been planted in 1882 on the banks of the Nooksack River in Northwestern Washington where it grew into a full-grown tree. The lives and events of the Nooksack Indians, as well as the area's first pioneers, passed before it.

Central to the exhibit was *The Tree Sculpture* (page 11). It was created by cutting a two-inch thick slab of wood from the entire length of the tree trunk and making it into boards. The boards, fashioned into ten bench tops, retained the irregular edge of the tree on both sides, and formed a continuous cross section of the tree from the base to the top. The lined up benches replicated the tree's trunk. Limbs and branches were suspended from above to recreate the canopy. The idea was to make it appear as though it first stood as a tree and then fell into furniture. The viewer could walk around the tree, experiencing its size, shape, what it once was, and what it had become.

This dramatic central display was surrounded by more than thirty other pieces of furniture built from the tree's wood, including a bedroom and dining room set, liquor cabinet, writing desk, and chair. On surrounding walls, a series of dynamic photos by Gunther José Frank, documenting the tree's harvest and its transformation into furniture, accompanied the exhibit.

A similar project had been undertaken and reported by groups of furniture makers in Tasmania and in England. They, too, had felled an old tree and distributed its parts to several wood workers who produced furniture, toys, utensils, and assorted other items. Gary Olson and Peter Toaig chronicle the English project in the book *One Tree,* listed in the bibliography.

Tools of the Trade

Lucky are today's wood workers who work in well-equipped studios with a wealth of power tools and hand tools. Even some hand tools are now powered by electricity. The furniture maker can drive screws with a power screwdriver, the sculptor can use a chain saw to fell trees and quickly block out and carve a sinuous form. The wood turner, who often used only a lathe to turn shapes, now may incorporate other tools such as a variety of saws, sanders, grinders, and whatever is necessary for accomplishing the task.

Along with saws, drills, and sanding equipment, there are planers, levelers, jointers, shapers, routers, measuring devices, and other specialized tools. One only has to survey the tool counters at home improvement stores, or wood workers' catalogs, to appreciate the array of tools available.

Many tools have gone digital, providing the wood worker more control of his medium with greater safety. Some are invented as the result of necessity. Dave Thompson of Seattle, Washington, mounted a laser pointer on his lathe that enables him to use the light beam for accurately judging the thickness of the walls of a turned vessel.

Despite mechanical tools and high tech equipment, traditional hand tools are also necessary for achieving many effects, and especially for carving and texturing a surface. These include chisels and gouges in different sizes, rifflers, rasps, files, and necessary sharpening equipment. Hand mallets in varying weights are also essential.

A native carver uses hand tools to carve a mask on an island in New Guinea. Wood carvers in primitive societies have no power tools, no well equipped shops, and yet they produce a prodigious amount of exciting work, often while sitting on the ground surrounded by one or more children. *Photo, Dona Meilach*

Nicola Henshaw works in her London, England, studio using a variety of hand carving tools for her unique furniture and sculpture shown elsewhere in the book. A pillar drill, sander, and saw can be seen in the background. *Photo, Mark Curzon*

Gregg Lipton shapes the leg for a table in his well-appointed studio. The unique building has been converted from a Civil War period water powered lumber mill in Cumberland, Maine. *Courtesy, artist*

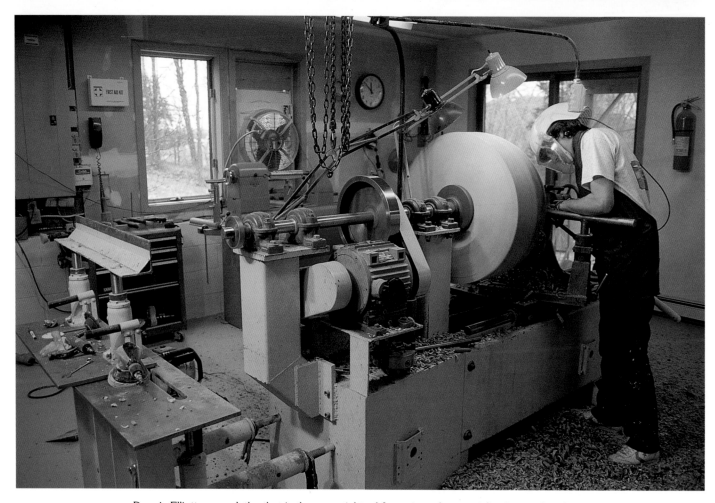

Dennis Elliott uses a lathe that is the essential tool for artists who specialize in woodturning. He hollows out a huge round form from a big leaf maple burl for a turned and sculptural vessel that will finally be 18" high and 24" diameter, and titled "Perigee." *Photo, Iona S. Elliott*

Clamps

In addition to tools for working directly with the wood, such as saws, drills, sanders, chisels and gouges, the woodworker, and especially the furniture maker, require a variety of clamps for holding together and gluing various joints. There are clamps for straight joints, for corners, mitered joints, and almost any type of gluing job that is required. If one doesn't exist, the intrepid woodwork can usually improvise or create exactly what he needs to solve a specific joining problem.

Wood Glues

Laminated woods, furniture joints, protrusions, assemblages almost always require some sort of adhesive. There are so many products on the market for so many different purposes, it's hard to know what will work well and permanently in a given situation. Most woodworkers learn by trial and error, by reading about glues, talking to the vendors where they buy their wood, and sharing experiences with other crafts people. Today, there's another way. Enter the term "wood glues/adhesives" into your Web browser and it will yield sites where you can enter the objects to be glued and receive a glue recommendation.

Colorants

Certainly, woods have inherent colors and people use and buy specific woods for their natural colors. However, many artists like to further enhance the woods. Some may use a non-descript wood and then purposely paint the entire surface. The type of colorant used will depend on the type of wood selected and the goals.

Safety

The importance of using tools properly and protecting eyes, ears, lungs, and face cannot be over emphasized. Carelessness and a cavalier attitude about using power tools, and even hand tools, can change your life in a second. Injure a hand, let a table saw slice your wrist, and whatever savings in time you might have gained, can result in untold anguish, and change your life dramatically.

Safety masks are a must when working with wood because of flying chips, and sawdust. For on-site in-doors work, where cutting, drilling or sanding is done, there must be exhaust fans with appropriate filters adjacent to the products being cut, drilled, or sanded, that will draw the dust away from the worker. Filters must be changed regularly and a store of replacement filters kept on-site at all times.

Certain woods may cause specific health problems. The woodworker should know what they are, how to deal with them, and to avoid woods that can cause reactions. For example, poplar can cause asthma, bronchitis, and dermatitis. Red cedar dust can give violent headaches, giddiness, stomach cramps, asthma, bronchitis, dermatitis, and irritation of the mucus membranes. If you're dealing with thorny yellowwood, lesions caused by thorns and splinters can take a long time to heal. Its dust causes dermatitis, cramps, eye and throat irritation, and vision disturbance.

Should someone experience allergies, or other abnormal effects from a given type of wood, the best idea is to stop using that particular wood. One should always have good ventilation, wear protective gloves, and wash hands before and after using a washroom. If you have to consult a health professional, be sure to acknowledge the work and materials you're using. Your symptoms, and the source of the problems, may be outside of a physician's everyday experience.

For further information on topics dealing with wood, use your Internet browser and pursue any of the following sites and their links:

Any type of wood by name
Forestry
Glues-adherents
Tree identification
Wood organizations (see Resource list in the Appendix)

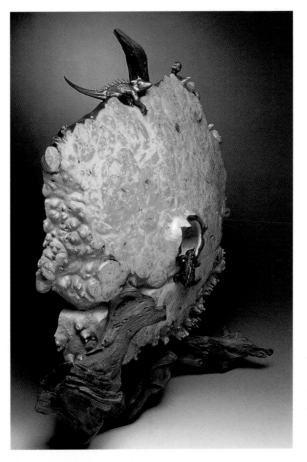

David Sengel. **Cliff Dwellers.** Maple burl, illustrates the random figuring in the burl wood compared to more regular figuring in cut board. The carved lizards are juniper and pear wood with rose thornbacks. 18" high, 16" wide, 4" deep. It's hard to maintain a preconceived idea of a form when working with a burl. The variations within the structure often dictate what the result will be. *Photo, artist*

John Makepeace. **English Fruits II**. A table in laminated limewood, carved and colored with artist's paints worked into the grain. Green Burlington slate top. Natural tree branches were used for the base. *Photo, Mike Murless*

Chapter 2
Furniture

Today is a great day to have a hand or interest in furniture as an art form. In rural and urban studios and workshops, talented artists are busy creating innovative designs and expressing art through the language of furniture.
Jonathan Benson

During the past few years, the term "studio furniture" evolved to describe one-of-a-kind pieces of furniture made in a studio as opposed to mass-produced manufactured furniture.

The person who creates studio furniture is an artist who pushes the potential of the medium and makes a new statement. Essentially studio furniture makers apply their design aptitude and talents to creating functional sculpture, for that is what studio furniture is.

I had covered this subject in two earlier books *Creating Modern Furniture, 1975,* and *Woodworking The New Wave,* 1981, Crown Publishers, and I was anxious to chronicle the changes I had observed. And dynamic changes there were in both form and style.

Mostly, these changes came from new talent. Many who had made their mark with innovative designs twenty to twenty-five years ago continue to work in a similar mode. Their recent work, well received by clients, is often a variation on a successful theme. A few of the artists who have published books covering their work declined invitations to submit photos for this book. This leaves ample room for new talent to be seen and discovered by an anxious and welcoming audience. I am pleased to showcase the work of talented artists who are making a place for themselves in the competitive milieu of contemporary studio furniture.

Today's studio furniture makers build hardwood tables, desks, chairs, cabinets, lamps, and mirrors emphasizing the artistic qualities of their materials. Some develop elegant, simple, restrained designs. Others dare to be different, flamboyant, and freewheeling. All seem to have bypassed traditional Queen Anne, and the gingerbread details of baroque and Victorian periods.

When woodworkers emulate designs from past historical periods, their pieces are beautifully crafted and functional. However, for this book, the aim was to find examples that went beyond what had been done before. If a designer borrowed elements from earlier furniture makers, the new designs had to have added another dimension, another look, to build upon familiar styles. John Makepeace's Table, *English Fruits II,* has a smooth top but the apron consists of hand carved fruit that might have grown from the tree base that supports the table. It represents an innovative approach to the traditional pedestal English table.

Fortunate is the furniture designer today who has the freedom to be conservative or outrageous, and takes advantage of that freedom. Buyers have learned to accept, and often seek, furniture that succeeds in standing out from pieces marketed by commercial manufacturers. Clients may seek an artist whose work they have admired at craft shows, at special studio furniture exhibits, in galleries, books, magazines, and on Internet sites.

The Internet has promoted artists' ability to display and sell unique work, and to bring together craftsperson and buyer in a nurturing relationship. Almost every artist whose work appears in this book can be located by entering his or her name in a WEB browser and some reference will appear. If it isn't that person's personal site, it will be part of an association, organization, or gallery that sponsors such sites. One has only to go to that site and find numerous links to others. Anyone unable to navigate the Internet can find a particular artist whose work appears in its pages by writing to the book publisher, the magazine editor, a gallery, or trade show management, and request a contact.

Artists need to have clients for their work. With proper showings and exposure, chances are they will. Studio furniture makers are entrepreneurs who expect to sell their work, and to find clients who will commission custom pieces. The fact of life for most crafts people is that they are artists first, and business people second. They would prefer to create art rather than spend time promoting and marketing. Still, they must cover their costs and make a profit.

It takes time to become known, to build, and maintain a reputation. Many artists also teach to support their more creative output. Artists whose work is shown in galleries, appear at art shows, and have a following, become visible and known. All of which helps to establish a career.

Tables

It is remarkable that the essential and seemingly simple form of a table has undergone dramatic changes over the past 25 years. Comparing "modern" tables made today with those in the earlier books illustrates radical differences. In *Creating Modern Furniture, 1975,* and *Woodworking the New Wave, 1985,* artists created tables that had curving, flowing elements made of heavily laminated steam bent wood parts.

Today's artists are making simpler designs with a greater emphasis on straight lines using the natural material in a more subdued manner. Gone is the use of wood for the sake of novelty in a table, a table base, the legs of a desk, or a chair. Now curved elements are natural, not contrived, not curved for the sake of being able to create a curve in wood, but rather to emphasize a joint, or a different direction in the basic form. Forced, curving table and chair legs are left to aluminum, plastic, iron, and materials that can more easily be formed into bent and bowed shapes. New materials such as glass, granite, plastic, acrylic, Corian and a variety of modern synthetics have become more popular. Fortunately, discriminating buyers will always favor fine wood tables because of the variety of textures, colors, durability, and sensual qualities associated with wood.

Meier Brothers. **Coffee Table.** The "cloth" is made of highly figured quilted maple. The frame and top corner are mahogany with an antique finish. One of a series of tablecloth tables from Meier Brothers that represents functional art. 27" high, 45" wide, 22" deep. *Photo, Sam Sargent*

Jo R. Roessler. **Dining table**. Cherry and walnut. Slats stored under the tabletop can be pulled out to seat 18 people. The design is inspired by traditional Asian architecture. Contemporary details and a striking wood combination give it a modern flair. 30" high, 72" long, 42" wide.
Courtesy, artist

Commercial factories supply mountains of furniture in non-descript designs or in period styles resurrected from past models. Art furniture makers may tap ideas from the past; but more likely, they derive their inspirations from their experiences, their individual interests, and from the materials.

After a first foray into making Taos style furniture in a Santa Fe, New Mexico factory, Jonathan Benson studied furniture design at different schools and was exposed to various stylistic influences. Eventually he developed his own style. He favors the geometric abstractions of Cubist and Futurist paintings for ideas. Today, he combines those ideas with the nature of the materials, incorporating burls and exotic woods into his pieces, and contrasting rough surfaces with unusual graining in the woods he selects.

Stephen Courtney's studio is a large warehouse space in an industrial site off a Los Angeles, California, main street. He favors unusual materials juxtaposing colored woods, unique textures, and hidden surprises of non-traditional materials and shapes in unexpected places. The cross-legged table (page 30) has B-B-shot under the glass, and a secretarial desk (page 73) incorporates golf tees. He describes his work as modern, progressive, dynamic, and different. 20th century architects and designers, such as John Lautner, influence him.

Mark Levin. **Jane Russell Leaf Hall Table**. Mahogany with walnut detailing. 30" high, 54" wide, 25" deep. *Photo, Margot Geist*

Mark Levin. **Georgi Mav Leaf Side Table.** Cherry with mahogany splines and Australian lace wood feet. 22" high, 46" wide, 25" deep. The artist shows how the table evolved in the following photo series. The table was named for an acquaintance who had died at an early age. *Photo series, Margot Geist*

Here's how the **Georgi Mav** table, previous page, was developed. The completed table, with the legs, weighs about 20 lbs.

1. Cherry wood is set up as four quadrants of laminated blocks. Each block is 4.5" thick.

2. The four quadrants are glued together with mahogany splines, and then cut to the table top shape.

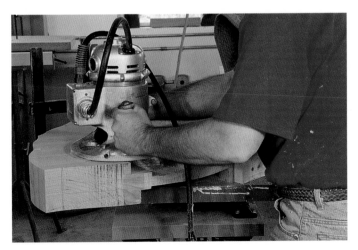

3. Before sculpting, the wood must be shaped and surfaced to produce a flat and usable top. It will be worked to approximately 7/8" thick.

4. The top and bottom are roughed out with a chain saw.

5. Levin uses files, rifflers, and other hand tools for the shaping.

6. The top and underside of the table are further sculpted. The three legs are tenoned and glued into the top. A pump drum sander is used to smooth and blend the legs into the top.

7. Final finishing requires about 25 hours of abrasive sanding. The piece is dry sanded to a 220 grit and wet sanded to a 400 grit, and then finished with Danish oil. *Series, courtesy Mark Levin*

David Holzapfel used the log itself for the table. Instead of constructing a base with legs built and attached to a top, he used the subtractive process, which he demonstrates in the series shown. He begins with a log cut to the height of the table he wants. He hollows out the interior, and subtracts additional areas to generate the form of the supporting base. The top is a piece of glass.

David Holzapfel. **Middle Management.** Spalted birch table with a Belgian St. Anne marble top. The base was carved with a chain saw. Details were added using hand tools and scorching techniques. 22" high, 26" diam. *Photo, artist*

David Holzapfel. **Katzman Dining Table.** Blister maple. The dark coloration is achieved by lightly scorching the surface with an acetylene torch. 29" high, 26" diam. *Photo, artist*

Here's how David Holzapfel created the **Katzman Dining Table** from a log:

1. A large tree trunk was cut to the size that would become the table height.

2. The interior was carved out with a chain saw.

3. After carefully measuring the circumference of the trunk the interlocking ovals were drawn on the cylinder.

4. Negative areas were removed, lines and edges trued, surfaces were finish-sanded, and then scorched. A final light sanding preceded finishing to result in the dining table on the facing page. *Series, courtesy, David Holzapfel*

Charles B. Cobb looks at table legs with a different eye, curving them and using only two legs to support a wall mounted hall table (page 29). John Makepeace's low table, *Rock,* (page 30) has sinuously curving lines around the outside and a secret central compartment. One could easily insert a vase within and have the plants appear to grow from the table's center.

Humor is in the table by Mark Sfirri; an endeavor that challenged him to deal with the mathematics posed in constructing it. His *Walking Table,* (Page 30), is an absolutely serious concept. Composed of spindle turned legs the table looks askew but only gives that impression from the twist of the legs on their axis.

Brent Skidmore also likes to introduce humor into his pieces. He strives to inject personality and uniqueness in the forms and in their relationship to one another. They are associated with the energies, emotions, and events that inspired the conception of the piece.

Brent Skidmore. **Faux Bamboo: Don't You Know?** Basswood, mahogany, African mahogany (sapele), leather, and a glass top. 18" high, 46" wide, 30" deep. *Collection, Rick and Dana Davis. Photo, David Ramsey*

James Betts. **Fives.** Veneer surface coffee table. Bees wing andiroba, satin wood, walnut, and curly maple. Betts' challenge was to create a non-geometric veneer design using random shapes. The five-sided form gave him that opportunity and the design evolved as he worked. 18" high, 41" long, 29" deep. *Photo, Melody La Montia*

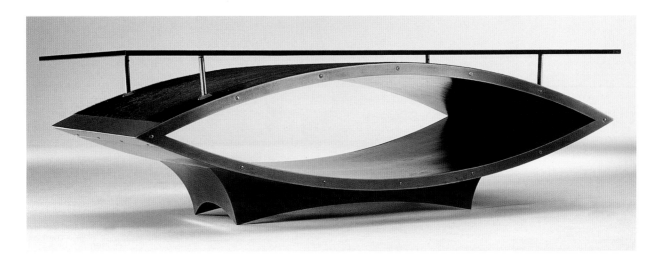

Top:
Jonathan Benson. **Constructivist Coffee Table.** Walnut and cherry wood with a granite top. Benson's designs often evolve from images in Cubist and Futurist paintings. 18" high, 42" wide, 22" deep. *Photo, James Hart*

Center:
Stephen Courtney. **Century Coffee Table.** Plywood form with applied maple wood veneer; fabricated steel elements on sides and face edges, and a steel base; all metal jitterbug treated, and pewter plated. There is leather beneath the floating glass top. 16.5" high, 53" wide, 30" deep. *Photo, artist*

Right:
Charles B. Cobb. **Demilune Hall Table.** Sepele veneer, bent plywood legs of quilted maple, and narra. The unique shaped legs were made on an ellipse guide cutter for a router. 36" high, 36" wide, 12" deep. *Photo, Hap Sakwa*

John Makepeace. **Rock.** Low table in English oak. It has a sculpted surround and a secret central compartment. Designed for a Cornish farmhouse close to the English coast. *Photo, Mike Murles*s

Mark Sfirri. **Walking Table.** Cherry and African wenge. Lathe turned spindles become the wobbly looking, but sturdy, legs for a table that is both practical and humorous. The objective was to create a sense of animation by adjusting the geometry of the axis to give the whole table a twist. 16" high, 24" square. *Collection, Los Angeles County Museum of Art, Los Angeles, California. Photo, artist*

Stephen Courtney. **Crossed Leg Table.** There's a metal bowl with B-B shot within that creates an unusual texture beneath the glass top. 18" high, 30" diam. *Photo, George Post*

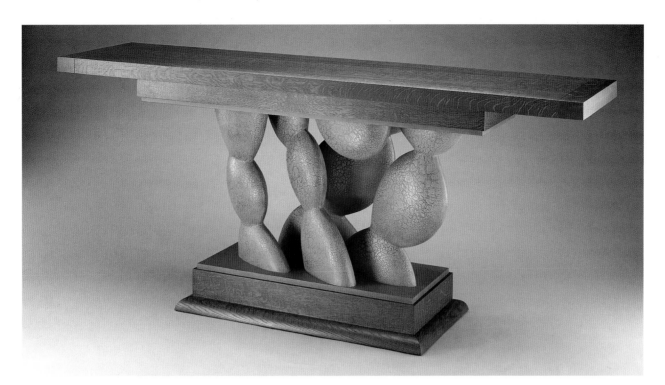

Wendell Castle. **The Missing Years**. Side table. Oak base and top. Sculpture "between" elements is polychromed orange. 36" high, 83.5" wide, 20" deep. *Courtesy, Leo Kaplan Modern Gallery, New York, New York.*

Victor DiNovi. **Tri-curve Display Table.** Koa. 40" high, 22" square. *Photo, artist.*

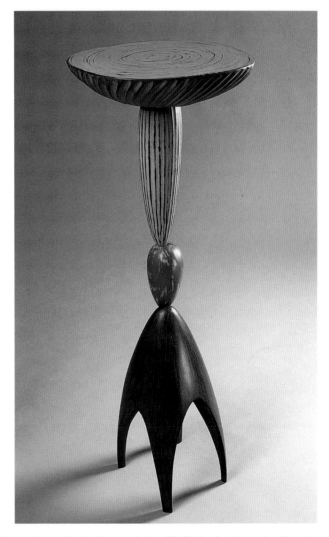

Derek Secor Davis. **Precambrian III.** Table. Poplar and milk paint. The concept was to use elemental forms in a sculptural manner, and not worry about the inherent color and grain of the wood. Color is achieved by combined scorching, carving, paint, and rubbing the paint through layers. 33" high, 12" wide, 11" deep. *Photo, artist*

31

John E. DeGirolamo. **BoLowe.** An entry table with a small drawer. Simple and clean styling. Walnut, curly maple, and ebony. 34" high, 50" wide, 12" deep. *Photo, artist*

Below:
John E. DeGirolamo. **BoLowe.** Detail of the drawer and tabletop. *Photo, artist*

Gregg Lipton. **Paulson Table**. Cedrino veneer, Swiss pear wood, and East Indian rosewood. The table was designed for a client who loved the transition of the leg to the top of his Gazelle table (page). The detailed version includes marquetry, inlay pinstripes, carved leg tops, and contrasting rosewood feet. Note the different treatment of the table's apron and the transition where it joins the legs compared to the original Gazelle table. Extends to 120" wide. *Photo, Jon Bonjour*

Gregg Lipton. **Paulson Table leg**. (Detail.) Swiss pear wood with East Indian rosewood pinstripe. Lipton's designs start with the legs, that are seamlessly united into the tabletop. Lipton says, "Innovation in furniture design is my ultimate objective. Finding unique solutions to age-old design problems— where to sit, to eat, to work, to relax, to sleep, to store—are my challenges and inspiration." *Photo, Jon Bonjour*

Gregg Lipton. **Gazelle Dining Table.** Curly maple and cherry. There are a matching serving table and coffee table. 30" high, 80" wide, 16" deep. *Photo, Stretch Tuemmler*

Gregg Lipton. **Gazelle Table leg.** (Detail.) By redesigning the cabriole style leg and contrasting it with a contemporary, thick, slab-like top the result is a "transitional" table that works well in contemporary, antique, and eclectic environments. Another nice feature of this table is the ample legroom under the top, a full 26.5 inches." *Photo, Stretch Tuemmler*

Gregg Lipton. **Courthouse Tables.** Cherry, slate, and steel. Two of seven litigant tables for the courthouse in Biddeford, Maine won as a Percent for Art Commission. Other pieces for the Courthouse included nine maple and steel built-in modern benches (page 49). Each is 30" high, 80" wide, 38" deep. *Photo, Dennis Griggs*

Gregg Lipton. **Torpedo Café Table** with **Circle-Back chairs**. The table has a steel base with an ebonized ash top. Lipton explains, "Although the outcome was very different and original, my chair plays on the equilateral triangle shape inspired by Frank Lloyd Wright's Prairie School style Barrel chair." Table: 30" high, 30" diam. Chairs: 36" high, 18" diam. *Photo, Dennis Griggs*

John Makepeace. **Sitwell.**
Brown oak, bog oak, and ash.
Four interlocking tables and
twenty chairs for a family dining
room. The elliptical table is
composed of four elements,
the two ends joining to seat
twelve, the center sections can
be used as side tables. The
chairs have sprung ash legs
and soft leather seats in four
different colors. *Photo, Mike
Murless*

Sam Maloof. **Table and chair
set.** This early furniture styling
set the tone for many of the
artist's later pieces, and helped
establish his reputation for
unique, simple, elegant, and
meticulously crafted one-of-a-
kind furniture. *Collection and
photo, John H. Ruble*

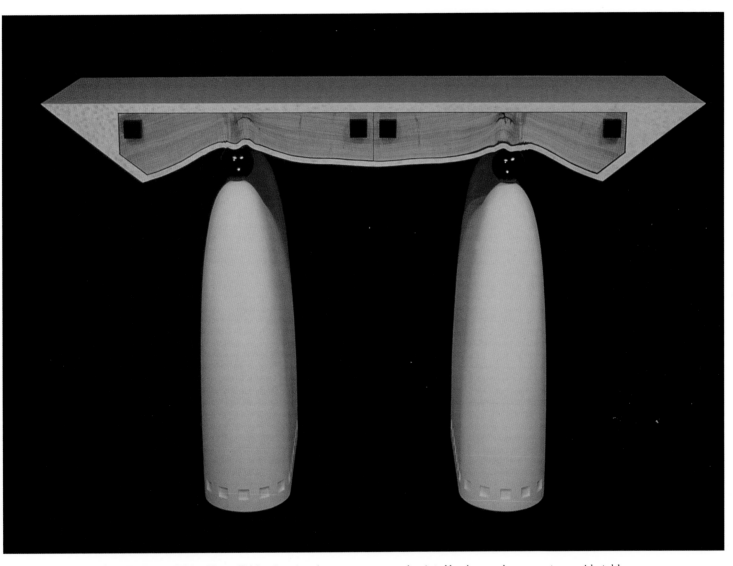

Charles B. Cobb. **White Mesa Table.** Acacia, ebony, veneers, and paint. May be used as an entry or side table. The drawer front was made from the natural edge of the wood and the table was designed around that shape. 36" high, 56" wide, 20" deep. *Photo, Ron Bath*

Craig Nutt's *Corn Table* is a pun on a pun. Corny, to say the least, but turning a common object into a table requires a wondrously warped sense of humor, and Nutt has it.

Nutt refers to himself as a "naturalized Southerner." He was born in Iowa where the tall corn grows. He has peeled back corn husks to form wings of airplanes such as the "Corncorde" he made for the Hartsfield Atlanta International Airport, Atlanta, Georgia. So using husks for the feet of this corn table came naturally.

Craig Nutt. **Tomato Table.** Oil paint on carved wood and a marquetry top with natural and dyed woods. Nutt started this table just as the first tomatoes of the season were begining to ripen and finished it as the last ones came off the vine. The feet are a balance of tomatoe leaves, traditional acanthus leafage, and a touch of high-heeled shoes. 26" high, 23" wide, 23" deep. Collection, Columbus Museum, Columbus, Georgia. *Photo, Ricky Yanaura*

Craig Nutt. **Corn Table.** Oil on carved wood. Curly maple top. The corn husks become the legs of a "traditional" tilt-top table. 23" high, 18" top diam. Collection, High Museum of Art, Atlanta, Georgia. *Photo, Ricky Yanaura*

Michael Ireland. **Steamshell.**
Olive ash burl dyed, gilded
wood, and hammered brass.
Glass top. A small dining table
that seats four. The center
piece is magnetized and
movable. It evolved as the
artist, doing vacuum bag
laminations, was searching for
more variety in shapes. The
result is a true cone, rather
than a cylindrical segment.
The idea was to show energy
flowing through the object
and represent the way he
creates. 30" high, 20" diam.
Photo, artist

Charles Cobb, Michael Creed, Nicola
Henshaw, and Michael Hosaluk look to
their surroundings in nature to pluck off
an idea for a unique and humor filled
table. Derek Secor Davis's *Illusions of
Grandeur* is like a personification of the
table and is itself a personification. Similar inspiration is used for other pieces of
furniture as fantasy, and fantastic ideas
occur when artists warm to their topic.

Charles B. Cobb. **"A" Table.** Powder coated
aluminum and mahogany. Laser cutting was
used to design the aluminum base. 1/2"
glass top. 24" high, 24" diam. *Photo, Hap
Sakwa*

39

Michael Creed. **Verdy Birdy.** Wood, copper, and paint. A drop wing table with a kinetic tail. A drawer lurks behind the figure on the front. The tongue serves as the drawer pull. 39" high, 36" wide. Collection, Bill and Gail Spiedel. *Courtesy, artist*

Nicola Henshaw. **Blue Crane Table.** Lime, oak, and steel. Henshaw often draws on stories and ideas from fables as her inspiration. Forms are taken from animals that she studies very closely. 32" high, 29" long, 24" deep. *Photo Mark Curzon*

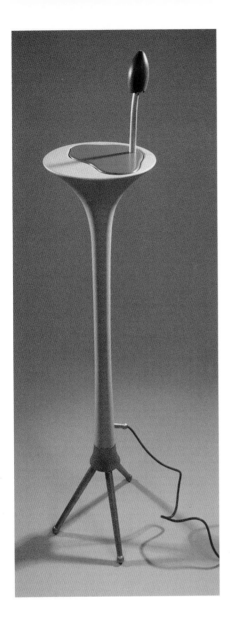

Brad Reed Nelson. **Poolside Paradise on a Pedestal**. Lamp table. Poplar, Osage orange, and aluminum. 34" high, 8" wide, 10" deep. *Photo, Alan McCoy*

Derek Secor Davis. **Illusions of Grandeur.** Recycled fir, pine, steel, and paint. The piece was reduced to its basic functional starting point and then frivolous sculptural decorations were added for a throne-like like appearance. 27" high, 23" square. *Photo, Maddog Studio*

Garry Knox Bennett. **Table lamp #14.** Wood, paint, steel, brass, and lamp parts. 51" high, 17.5" wide, 29.5" deep. *Leo Kaplan Modern Gallery, New York. Photo, artist*

Joël Urruty. **Untitled.** Coffee Table. Mahogany and Ash. Urruty explains, "The idea behind this glass top coffee table is to have it jump out at you. The table is an organic plant-like form that appears to be growing right through the glass top. I design my furniture to have a sense of movement and to contradict that historical notion that furniture is heavy and inanimate. My tables create the illusion that they are either growing, tipping over, or walking away from you. *Photo, Pat Simione*

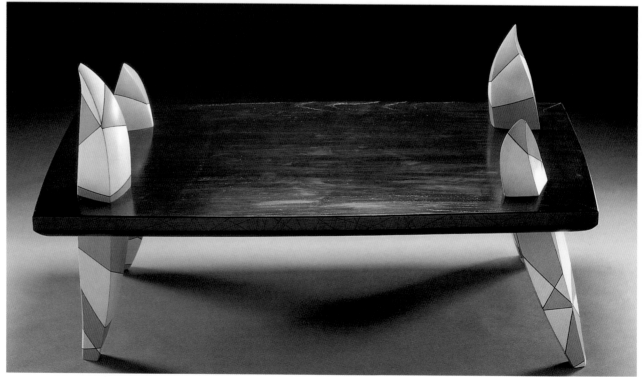

Michael Hosaluk. **Unusual Fruit Tables.** Painted wood, copper, hair, and acrylic gel. These tables are a result of encounters with nature and people They possess humor and gesture; with references to culture and our social ideological lives. They create balance with imbalance. 25" high, 26" wide, 16" deep. *Photo, Grant Kernin*

Seating

Most of us spend a great portion of our lives sitting in some form of a chair from the time we wake up until we go to bed. We may sit on a bench at a vanity, at a chair or stool while we eat breakfast, at a desk while we work at school or around a boardroom table, and in a car seat. We relax in a chair at the theatre, or on a couch in front of the television— you get the idea. The ergonomics of the chair has come into sharp focus since the computer age when people began spending long hours bent and almost immobilized in a seated position while staring into a monitor. Then all kinds of new physical problems arose including back pain, neck pain, and wrist ailments. For many of these problems, the chair has been the culprit. Therefore, a chair Holy Grail was, and still is, being sought.

The examples of seating that follow will not necessarily end the search for comfort seating magic but they will provide an insight into how artists are creating chairs today. There are the simple and not so simple bench, the rocker, desk chair, dining chair, pull-up chair and the outdoor chair. What are the design inspirations for these chairs? Often they are based on historical concepts updated. Certainly, they are around in profusion. The history of the chair is a study in itself and most of us can conjure an image when we mention Egyptian, Windsor, Queen Anne, Victorian, Shaker, Craftsman, Frank Lloyd Wright, and other chair styles.

Today's studio furniture makers more likely block those images from their minds and try to create a new style based on today's needs, on a client's vision, on a composite from another artist's vision, on an animal, a plant, or a fantasy.

The chairs made by today's studio furniture makers, and the names of the makers themselves, are building a niche in history. Surely today's generation of designers is creating the collectibles of tomorrow. You'll find that history in the making in the photos in this chapter.

What are the qualifications that make a chair outstanding and a candidate in the line of history?

It must be an art form able to stand alone, or be combined with other furniture to become a sculpture in space. It should have a simplicity in balance and proportion, have a purity of line and form, be comfortable, and functional.

Nicola Henshaw. **Duck Bench.** (Detail.) Carved oak and steel. After carving, the benches are stained in appropriate, and sunlight fast colors. They are on the Grounds of Colchester Hospital, London, England. 32" high, 79" long, 40" deep. *Photo, Andra Nelki*

Opposite page:
Nicola Henshaw. **Peacock Carved Bench**. Oak and steel. Colchester Hospital entrance, London, England. Henshaw's bench takes its cue and inspiration from the peacocks that are a prominent feature of the area on which the hospital is sited. Some benches have sculptures of the familiar ducks and geese on the nearby lake. 52" high, 79" long, 40" deep. *Photo, Andra Nelki*

Tai Lake. **Significant Other Bench**. Matched koa wood. This was a departure from the artist's usual chairs. It earned several awards at shows. *Photo, Ranagh Productions*

Benches

The slab bench is one of the simplest seating forms there is. Essentially, it consists of a flat slab supported by two upright slabs or four legs, or perhaps a middle support, depending on its length and the strength of the slab. Many benches also have backs. The park bench in wood or metal, for example, is pervasive. Spin-off designs of that classic model are used indoors and out.

A bench is often considered "temporary seating." An example is Gregg Lipton's courthouse bench that serves people who must wait. A bench is more tolerable for such waits than standing in line. Modern interior designers know that a bench can be designed to blend with the architecture of a building and the styles of other furniture. They are not afterthoughts plunked down where and when needed. Lipton's benches are coordinated with tables he created for the courthouse in Biddeford, Maine.

Nicola Henshaw's unique benches have a fascinating background. She worked as an artist in residence in Bangalore, India, for three months. While there, she made several pieces of furniture for the grounds of the Himatsingka Seide silk factory. There was the peacock, the duck, and also a chicken and an elephant bench. She patterned the chicken on the comical India chickens always seen busily running around along the roadsides. Since then, she has made several bird benches.

Garry Knox Bennett's bench, with the hard round form at each end, is a take off of the African headrest. One could use the bench for seating as well as stretching out and supporting the head or feet.

Meier Brothers. **High Back Settee**. Seats three. Highly figured quilted maple for the frame. Back insets are highly figured African rosewood. 42" high, 54" wide, 20" deep.
Photo, Tony Grant

R.A. Laufer. **Still Pond Bench for Two.** Walnut. Wave shaped top and raised inset ambrosia maple seat. 18" high, 48" wide, 14" deep.
Photo, Deborah Jeon

Dennis Theisen. **Bench.** Black walnut, galvanized corrugated steel, joined and fabricated. *Courtesy, artist*

Kelli Kiyomi Kadokawa. **George and Vida.** Sitting bench. Poplar, quarter-sawn oak, salt cedar, and paint. 31" high, 58" wide, 17" deep. *Photo, Conrad Eek*

Victor DiNovi. **Tete-a-tete Bench**.
Walnut. 21" seating height, 52" wide,
34" deep. *Photo, artist*

Gregg Lipton. **Benches for the
Biddeford, Maine, Courthouse**.
Maple and steel. Each bench is 38"
high, 80" wide, 23" deep. *Photo,
Dennis Griggs*

Garry Knox Bennett. **African Bench**. Walnut, PVC, and paint. Inspired by the headrests in African furniture. 33"
high, 67" wide, 20" deep. *Leo Kaplan Modern Gallery, New York, New York. Photo, M. Lee Fatheree*

Derek Secor Davis. **Bench with Two Stones.** Koa, poplar, milk paint, and concrete. The seat is a basically a large, rustic, rough sawn plank with sculptural edges. It suggests the essence of wood, but Davis likes to have his furniture hold something, so he carved a bowl form and put two hand carved wood "stones" within. When people handle them, they are surprised because they are so light. 19" high, 66" wide, 21" deep. *Photo, courtesy, artist*

Meredith Sattler. **Continuum Bench**. Birch plywood, and dye. The bench is an experience of space and time in which humans become, and experience, pieces of an individual puzzle. 11.5" high, 46" wide, 14" deep. *Photo, John Dickey*

Rick Pohlers. **Benches.** The larger bench is fiddleback maple and African wenge. The gently curving shapes and the joinery detailed legs are for structure, color, and visual appeal. 17" high, 45" wide, 16" deep. The smaller bench is bubinga. 17" high, 24" long, 16" deep. *Photo, Richard Hines*

Joël Urruty. **Freestyle Bench.** Basswood and milk paint. He views his benches as horizontal sculptures that allow great freedom in working with form. Large heavy benches with visual mass and weight have a wonderful permanent presence inviting the audience to sit down without any worries. 18" high, 60" wide, 24" deep. *Photo, Pat Simione*

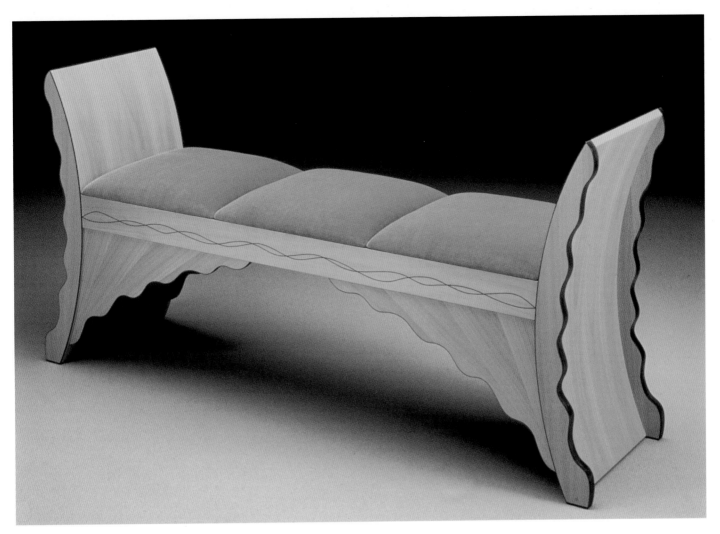

Jamie Robertson. **Water Bench.** East Indian rosewood and lemonwood veneers, bending birch, and cherry woods. Lacquer finish. Upholstered cushions. The idea was to capture the refreshing spontaneity of a splash of water and a breaking wave. 27" high, 58" wide, 16" deep. *Photo, artist*

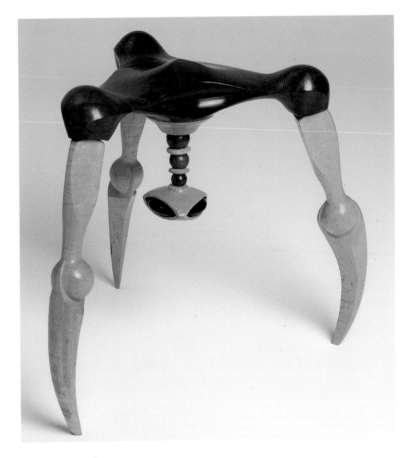

Michael J. Brolly. **Looking for Love in All the Wrong Places.** Stool. Maple, walnut, and a spring. 22" high, 23" wide, 21" deep. *Photo, David Haas*

Sam Maloof. **Rocker**. Walnut and ebony. Maloof's rocker has become a classic design. He's been making them for more than 30 years and they have become collector's items. *del Mano Gallery, Los Angeles, California. Photo, Gene Sasse Inc.*

Rockers

Through the years, wooden rocking chairs have gone through several iterations. Early American rockers had mostly flat seats and spindle backs. Swedish rockers, called *gungstols*, were made until the early 1900s. In England, the Windsor rocker had a back frame shaped like a hoop. It was introduced to the American Colonies around 1740. A birdcage rocker without armrests was used around 1800 and a high back Boston rocker with arms appeared about 1840. There was a Salem rocker, and a Shaker rocker about 1820, and Adirondack rockers in many shapes from about the 1830s. None of these conformed to the human body.

In 1950, Sam Maloof began making rockers that set new standards in design, technical mastery, and comfort. His signature walnut rockers are visually elegant, comfortable, and enduring with long graceful ski-like rockers that curve inward at the back like an antelope's horns. Other furniture makers are also contributing to the customized body shaped rockers. Gregg Lipton's, and Tai Lake's rockers are heralding a new approach to the comfortable and beautiful rocking chair.

Gregg Lipton. **Rocker.** Cherry. Lipton challenges age old traditional designs. In this rocking chair he deviates from current rocker styles and constructs a unique solution to the rocker concept. 42" high, 24" wide. 43" deep.
Photo, Stretch Tuemmler

Tai Lake. **Lunch With Frank.** Koa wood is from a forestry project that he manages in Kona, Hawaii. 42" high, 23" wide, 46" deep. *Photo, Rana Productions*

John Nyquist. **Inclined Rocking Chair.** Figured maple with rosewood accents. The spindles are carved to fit the body contour. Seat is upholstered in Jack Lenor Larsen wool fabric. 46" high, 27" wide, 38" deep. *Courtesy, artist*

Rick Pohlers. **Rocking Chair**. California walnut and fiddleback maple. 45"
high, 48" wide, 23.5" deep. *Photo, Richard Hines*

John Makepeace. **Trine II**. Chair in yew, bog oak side, and painted detailing. The seat and back are made in alternate layers of yew (2 mm), and bog oak (1 mm). The legs and arms are comprised of laminated yew, bent and spiraled around the body. *Photo, Mike Murliss*

Pull-up Chairs

Pull-up chairs, that is chairs that one can pull up to a table, a desk, or just move around in a lounge, on a porch, or a den, are lightweight and considered "portable." Mostly they are made of wood but often the wood is combined with other materials. Today, such chairs may be made of alumi-num, iron, molded plastic, and other materials. In these examples, wood is the dominant material.

A chair, first of all, should be comfortable. That's a tall order because different people will find comfort in a variety of chairs for short periods. They should be well designed, and as required for inclusions in this book, the pieces should be sculptural and functional.

Victor DiNovi. **Dining Chair.**
Mahogany. *Photo, artist*

Jo R. Roessler. **Wood Office Chair.** A
conundrum of angles and joints, this
chair is a favorite among architects
and engineers. Solid wood and
classical joinery make for a sturdy
and visually exciting chair. Maple or
cherry. *Photo, Courtesy, artist*

Dennis Theisen. **L-Chair.** Laminated and bent plywood with cocobolo veneers, and rolled and welded steel. 21" high, 37" wide, 27" deep.

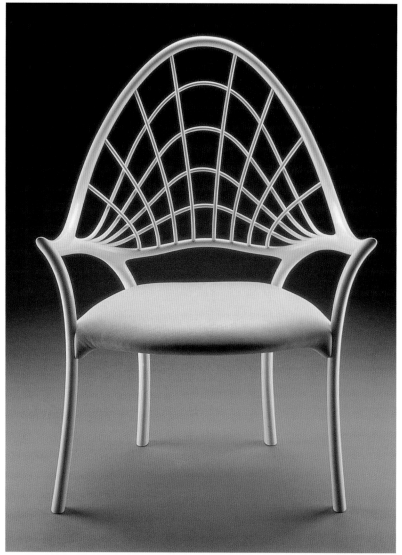

John Makepeace. **Millennium Chair.** Each component is built up from sequential layers of holly wood in a two-part "spiral" jig. The elements are then joined by splicing and pinning them where they cross. These chairs are in the Lewis Collection, Richmond, Virginia, and the Art Institute of Chicago, Chicago, Illinois. *Photo, Mike Murliss*

Gregg Lipton. **Circle back chairs**. Bleached ash. 36" high, 18" wide, 18" deep. *Photo, Stretch Tuemmler*

Kurt A. Nielsen. **Madonna Chairs**. Walnut, mahogany, leather, and brass nails. When one sits in the chairs their head is framed by the halo; They appear as though they are in a Byzantine portrait of the Virgin Mary. *Photo, David Ramsey*

Dennis Theisen. **Cable Chair.** Cherry wood, turned, and shaped. Painted steel tubing, cable, and hardware, fabricated. 32" high, 14" wide, 18 " deep. *Photo, Courtesy artist*

Dennis Theisen. **Dancing Chair.** Walnut crotch veneer on laminated and bent mahogany. Welded and painted rebar. 17" high, 18" wide, 12" deep. *Courtesy, artist*

John Makepeace. **Serendipity Chair**. A limited edition chair made in a choice of woods with aluminum and leather. The cast and polished aluminum back and arms encourage good posture and comfort over long periods. *Photo, Mike Murless*

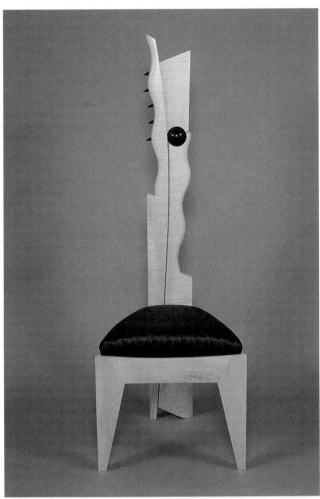

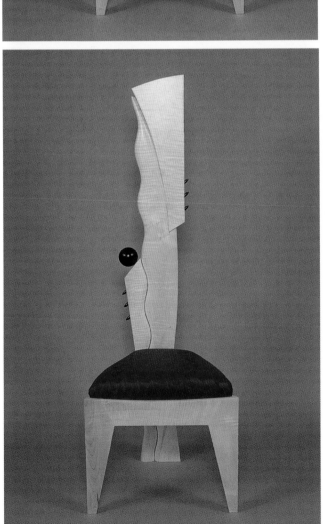

Charles B. Cobb. **Sculptchair #2.** Bleached maple and African wenge, with fabric. These chairs are answers to his question, "What can you do with sculpture?" Sit on it. 60" high 21" diam. *Photo, Ron Bath*

Chris Martin. **Pine Needles Valet Chair.** Redwood burl, maple, and steel. Inspired by the conifers in Colorado and his attraction to beautiful woods from his own area. 72" high, 20" diam. *Photo, artist*

Charles B. Cobb. **Sculptchair #3.** Bleached maple and African wenge, with fabric. He says, "I designed twenty of these but have made only five so far." 60" high 21" diam. *Photo, Ron Bath*

Nicola Henshaw. **Cat Chair.** Carved lime. A clever use of an animal image. Is it a cat with two heads or two, two legged cats, each with a tail?. The symbolism works. It is attention getting, amusing, practical, and sculptural. 32" high, 20" wide, 20" deep. *Photo, Mark Curzon*

Michael Creed. **Nesting Instinct.** A combination seat, kinetic coat rack, and hall tree. Walnut with painted leather upholstery. 92" high, 43" wide. *Collection, R. L. Deal.Courtesy, artist*

Michael Hosaluk. **Cactus Chair.** Painted wood. The spikes stick out everywhere but where you sit, making it apprehensive for seating. Once you sit, it is very comfortable but you remain cautious. The idea is to have the work stimulate your sense and communicate an underlying narrative. 42" high, 22" wide, 18" deep. *Photo, artist*

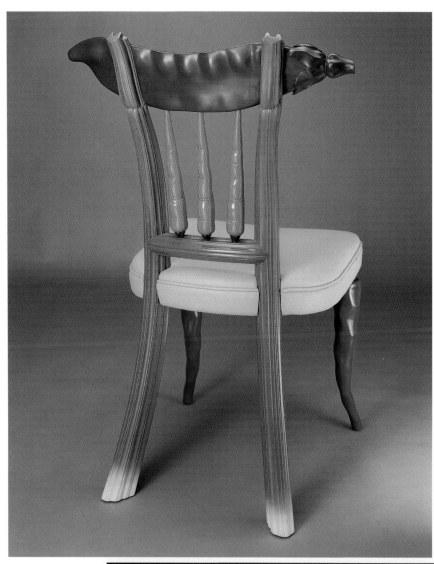

Craig Nutt. **Celery Chair with Peppers, Carrots, and a Snow Pea**. The rear legs are celery and the other images are obvious. Painted wood. "The Celery Stalks presented an unexpected design challenge," says Nutt, "how to make the joints work without reinforcing them with peanut butter or cream cheese." The chair is actually quite comfortable and, according to Nutt, if you lean back you can massage your back with the peas. *Photo, Rickey Yanaura*

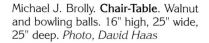

Michael J. Brolly. **Chair-Table**. Walnut and bowling balls. 16" high, 25" wide, 25" deep. *Photo, David Haas*

Andrew Muggleton. **Balustrade Chaise**. Brushed aluminum curved areas are secured to lace wood supports on a beautifully curved African wenge base. The headrest is upholstered in Ultra-suede. 29" high, 59" long, 20" deep. *Pismo Gallery, Denver, Colorado. Photo, Artist*

John E. DeGirolamo. **Modirondack.** Outdoor chairs are constructed of water resistant Medium Density Fiberboard (MDF), poplar, and paint. The indoor models are water resistant MDF, maple and paint. The Modirondack chair is a "MOD"ern twist on the classic Ad"IRONDACK" chair. The chair melds the casual function of the classic Adirondack into a flowing modern form that is equally at home on the beach or in a stylish loft. They can be pushed together to form a bench or grouped in designer colors to create a contemporary, symmetrical effect. 29" high, 24" wide, 40" deep. *Courtesy, artist*

John Makepeace. **Bird**. Burr elm, cast bronze, wych elm, and leather. A personal desk. From the cast bronze foot, the column supports the cantilevered surface that contains the curved drawers that wrap around as they open. The adjustable angle writing surface has four trays that swivel out for easy access. *Photo, Mike Murless*

Desks

The word desk usually refers to furniture at which one sits and works or writes. Today there is also the "help" desk that may not be a desk at all; rather it's a symbol of a place where one can get help for a computer or other problem. The computer has changed the concept of a virtual desk. It becomes the support for the unit that accomplishes what one traditionally does on a desk. The computer may require a desk to hold it, but it could also sit on a stand or a table. The laptop computer requires the lap as its desk. Therefore, the concept of the desk has changed and its form depends on its purpose, and where it is in a room.

Generally, an office desk is more massive than a home secretarial desk. The secretarial desk is smaller in scale, daintier and more highly styled than an office desk. Despite these many variations, a desk remains an essential furniture piece with a flat top, legs, and, usually, drawers or some system for holding papers.

Beyond that, the style may differ greatly. We know what many desks of yore looked like from prints, photographs, paintings, wall drawings, and friezes. We can see styles from ancient Greece, Rome, the 17th to 19th centuries in France, and recent history. We know the roll top desk was popular in early America because we see it pictured in many western movies. Its thin slatted sliding top could be pulled, or rolled, down to cover the work surface. The tambour desk, with its French heritage, had a solid rounded cover that could be pulled down to hide the desk's surface. Both could be locked for security and secrecy. Today's designers may employ these traditional elements but in much different ways and in a variety of styles.

John Makepeace's *Bird Desk*, Jefferson Shallenberger's *Writing Desk*, and Roger Heitzman's *Arch Desk* have the curved line as major design elements. Heitzman's *Bubinga Desk* is rectilinear but all edges have been softened and smoothed into flowing curves.

Stephen Courtney's *Secretarial Desk* is also a symphony of curves but it has a theme. It might be more aptly titled a desk for the golfing executive. The rounded top surface is covered with golf tees kept in place under a sheet of curved glass. Courtney points out that the front two legs are as-

Jefferson Shallenberger. **Writing Desk**. Narra and black palm. The wood's semicircular natural graining sets the theme for the repeat curves in the piece. 22" high, 42" wide, 22" deep. *Photo, artist*

sembled to the body with golf balls. The interior is beautifully finished and looks like a Greek temple with columns and architectural detailing. It is now in the collection of the Renwick Gallery of the Smithsonian Museum in Washington, D.C.

Derek Secor Davis shows how a desk is built in a series of photos that can help one appreciate how much work and precision are involved in creating a desk.

Gregg Lipton's *Gazelle Desk* illustrates unusual detailing while Kurt Nielsen's desks demonstrate his affinity for combining different colored woods. The Meier Brothers *Executive Desks* ooze with a feeling of love for their work, and how wood can be made into beautifully sculptured functional art. Michael Creed's desks are loaded with imagery and symbolism.

Roger Heitzman. **Arch Desk**. Bubinga. The organizer has 3 drawers; the desk body has one wide drawer with pulls carved from the solid wood front. 50" high, 67" wide, 28" deep. *Photo, artist*

Stephen Courtney. **Secretarial Desk**. Solid stock maple
hardwood; maple golf tees beneath bent glass, cast metal, and
a copper plated detail. The writing surface is leather with
copper leafing; The 2000 maple wood golf tees on the curved
top surface beneath the glass are for texture and interest. 48"
high, 43" wide, 23.5" deep. *Collection, The Renwick Gallery of
the Smithsonian Museum, Washington, D.C. Photo, artist*

Detail of front corner showing the
golf ball, leg construction, and the
golf tees along the top. *Photo, artist*

Kurt A. Nielsen. **Wave Desk and Whale Chair**. Australian lace wood, quilted maple, and cherry. A commissioned piece inspired by overlooks at the Atlantic Ocean. The chair back is shaped like a whale's tail. The desk is 30" high, 66" wide, 32" deep. *Photo, David Ramsey*

Kurt A. Nielsen. **Gregory Desk**. Australian lace wood, quilted maple, maple, and cherry. 30" high, 72" wide, 34" deep. *Photo, David Ramsey*

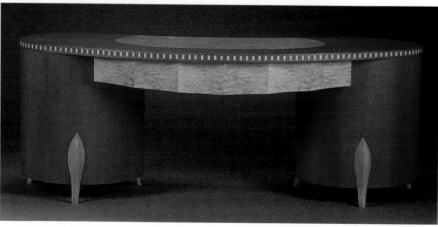

Kurt A. Nielsen. **Gregory Desk**, back view. *Photo, David Ramsey*

Roger Heitzman. **Bubinga Desk**. Bubinga. Two continuous sculpted curves across the desk front double as drawer pulls. Though the desk is rectangular, it is replete with curves on every element. 45" high, 60" long, 36" deep. *Photo, artist*

Derek Secor Davis. **Writing Desk.** Cherry maple burl. Secor tries to avoid straight lines as much as possible. This desk's high tech look resembles the cockpit of an airplane. 37" high, 66" wide, 31" deep. *Photo, Maddog Studio*

Derek Secor Davis shares the ideas, planning, and creating of his *Secretary Desk* in the photos that follow. The desk uses traditional joinery but it has a floating flying feeling much like one might experience in front of an airplane control panel. He likes rounded, curvilinear, slender forms that give the piece a light, airy feel. Great attention is paid to the ergonomics and function of the organizational spaces. Drawers and slots are designed to be handy and aesthetically exciting.

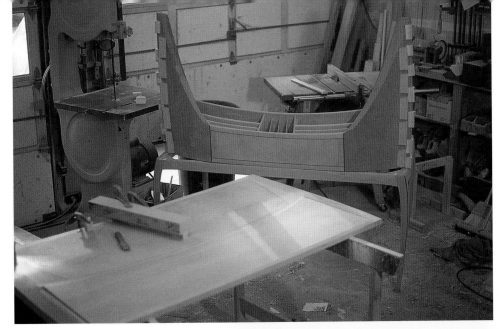

Derek Secor Davis shows construction and assembly procedures for his writing desk. He assembles the base, then the top will be positioned and glued to the base. *Photo series, courtesy, artist*

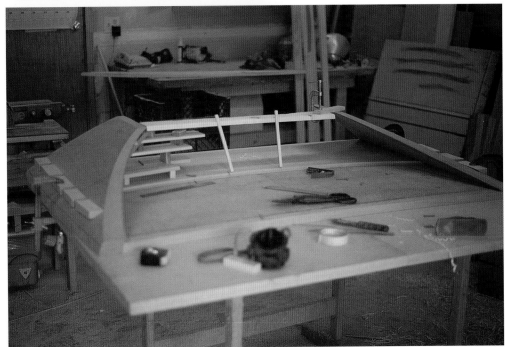

The insides of the desk have to be cut, fitted, and assembled within the top part of the desk. Davis is acutely aware of the ergonomics of organization, and he designs the negative spaces for efficiency.

Gluing and clamping require very careful planning. Each section has to be glued and clamped in a pre-planned order. It requires such precision that a dry run is required to be sure all parts will be done in the planned consecutive order within a prescribed time frame allowing for the glue to set.

Meier Brothers. **Executive Desk** has two file drawers, two drawers for papers, and a spacious desktop. The top and drawer fronts are figured walnut on a walnut frame. Sides and accents are highly figured quilted maple. 30" high, 72" wide, 32" deep. *Photo, Sam Sargent*

Meier Brothers. **Executive Desk,** detail.

Meier Brothers. **Executive desk** with two drawers and pen and pencil holders. Hidden compartments provide safe spots for valuables. The desk is fiddleback walnut on a black walnut frame. Accents are fiddleback maple. Desk is 30" high, 72" wide, 32" deep. *Photo, Tony Grant*

Meier Brothers. Detail.

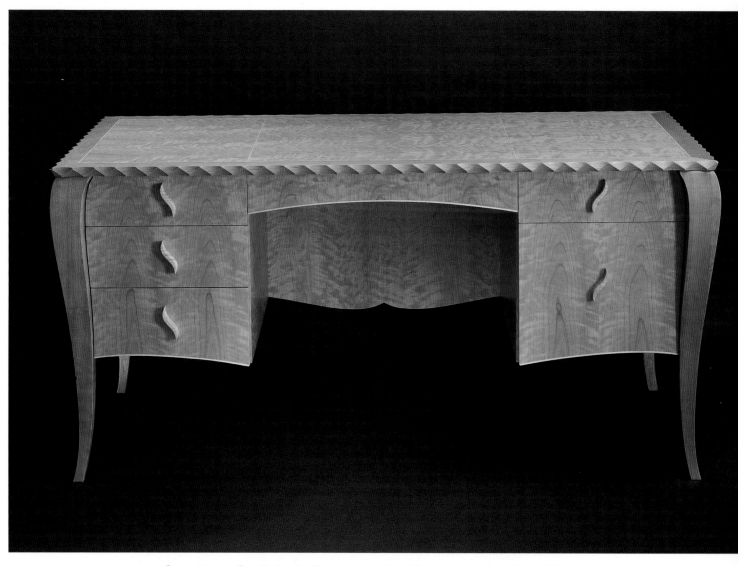

Gregg Lipton. **Gazelle Desk.** Cherry and maple, with a scalloped edge band. 30"
high, 68" wide, 28" deep. *Photo, Stretch Tuemmler*

Garry Knox Bennett. **Pear Desk with Bench**. Curly maple, leather, glass, and paint. 30" high, 73" wide, 37" deep. *Leo Kaplan Modern Gallery, New York, New York. Photo, M. Lee Fatheree*

Stephen Courtney. **Three-Legged Desk**. Solid stock maple hardwood legs; plywood form with maple wood veneer. In contrast to the desks based on the curving line, in this desk Courtney relies on geometric shapes and angles. Stainless steel knobs; legs/foot details. 30" high, 48" wide, 24" deep. *Photo, artist*

Michael Creed. **Owls and Pussycats Post Office.** A lady's writing desk. Cherry wood, walnut, quilted maple, leather, and paint. 42" high, 44" wide, 24" deep. *Courtesy, artist*

Michael Creed. **Owls and Pussycats Post Office.** (Detail) *Courtesy, artist*

Garry Knox Bennett. **Owl Desk with Chair**. Honduras mahogany, rosewood, California walnut, brass, gold plate, and paint. The rear interior is illuminated. 53" high, 73" wide, 37" deep. *Photo, M. Lee Fatheree*

Michael Ireland. **Tut.** Nicknamed, **The Scotchball**. It is a motorized and remote controlled liquor cabinet. Its inspiration is the art deco home bars in movies from the thirties. When a door opens, a shelf slides out and bottles pop up. Mahogany, gilded wood, hammered brass, polychrome wood, and fabric. Elements that appear as metal are wood that has been carved and painted to appear metallic. *Photo, artist*

Roger Heitzman. **Art Deco Credenza**. Twelve species of wood are used, plus aluminum. The two curved, laminated doors and two drawer fronts feature veneer marquetry designs. Comparing the Art Nouveau buffet and the Art Deco designs clearly illustrates the different elements in the two design styles. 32" high, 50" wide, 22" deep. *Photo, artist*

Roger Heitzman. **Art Deco Credenza,** open. Art Nouveau relies on curves inspired by plants and natural forms. Art Deco appeared later. It is more geometric and angular incorporating straight lines inspired by the Mayan architecture that was discovered in the early 1920s. *Photo, artist*

Kurt A. Nielsen. **Guardian Dog Credenza**. Maple, madrone burl, and linden wood. The shelf is cleverly supported by a wing on each of the two carved dogs. There are two drawers below. Inspiration for this piece was a Manhattan neighbor's Chihuahua that sported a dog-size black Harley jacket. 48" high, 60" wide, 16" deep. *Photo, David Ramsey*

By his own admission, Kurt A. Nielsen's furniture is hard to describe. One thing is absolute; it is never overlooked or ignored. He says, "With every piece, I aim to create an environment in which the viewer is enticed to participate." He blends classical furniture forms that invoke nostalgia and timelessness, with carved, fanciful guardians designed to stir the imagination."

Nielsen thinks of his works as reliquaries, whether he's creating furniture, sculpture, or both. These reliquaries hold the user's precious objects or memories. Guardians may be represented literally or as abstract animal forms that may come from dreams, mythology, architecture, Classic Greek, and Roman sculpture, or even Saturday morning cartoon characters. His pieces are never boring and the craftsmanship is exquisite.

Kurt A. Nielsen. **Guardian Dog Credenza**. Detail illustrates the stylized form and the hand carving. *Photo, David Ramsey*

Kurt A. Nielsen **Minotaur Morning.** Honduras mahogany, pommelle sapele, African satinwood, and 14K gold. Nielsen says he aims to make furniture that gets noticed, is seldom overlooked, and stirs people's interest. 32" high, 34" wide, 21" deep. *Photo, David Ramsey*

Kurt A. Nielsen. **Minotaur Morning**. (Detail of the Minotaur.) Nielsen likes to hand blend classical furniture forms with fanciful guardians. Often his pieces have hidden compartments. The carved fanciful guardians may be a reliquary for holding precious items. *Photo, David Ramsey*

Kurt A. Nielsen. **Adam and Eve Secretary and Media Cabinet**. Note the snake used for the handle to carry out the theme. 68" high, 46" wide, 25" deep. *Photo, David Ramsey*

Kurt A. Nielsen. Detail of Adam with his hand out-stretched offering the apple to Eve. *Photo, David Ramsey*

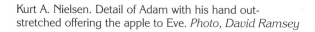

Chris Martin. **Queen Anne's Alter Ego**. White oak, brown oak burl, copper leaf, and forged steel. This commissioned media cabinet holds a stereo system along with drawers to hold CD's, DVD's, and videos. 26" high, 52" wide, 21" deep. *Photo, artist*

Chris Martin. **Quilted Chest**. White oak, cedar, floor tile, and bronze. This piece was tricky because it involved new problems and solutions. There are no single right angles or flat surface to the piece. It is cedar lined, and the top is composed of cut and shaped linoleum floor tiles. 19" high, 37" wide, 25" deep. *Photo, artist*

Chris Martin, John Makepeace, Gregg Lipton, and Jefferson Shallenberger use shapes that are more traditional but push the envelope so that it opens in new directions. Charles Cobb probably never thought of making a cabinet with a straight outer line. Brent Skidmore adroitly combines lines and curves in new relationships that evoke a smile from the viewer. That's fine with Skidmore who strives to show awkward relationships, and the use of color to help him "celebrate humor" as a strong and healing elixir.

Brent Skidmore. **Ripple**. Mahogany, poplar, and Medium Density Fiberboard. 41" high, 39" wide, 13" deep. Collection, David Ramsey. *Photo, David Ramsey*

Brent Skidmore. **Ripple**. Detail of the back of the cabinet. Photo, David Ramsey

Wendell Castle. **Rocky's Dream.** Jelutong and white oak. Blanket or sweater storage chest, or a hope chest. The painted bright red inside lifts and is hinged at the back. 41" high, 71" wide, 24" deep. *Courtesy. Leo Kaplan Modern Gallery, New York, New York*

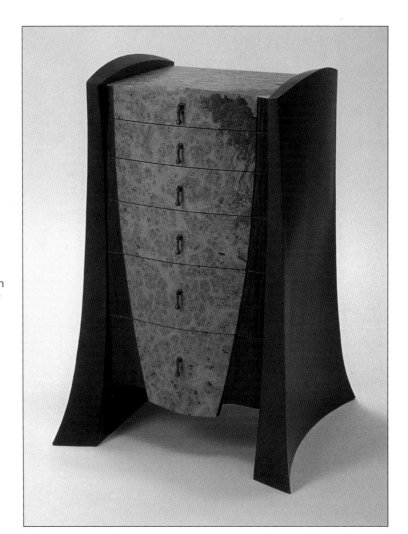

Chris Martin. **Monolith Chest**. White oak burl, other woods, and steel. Finding a large enough burl was lucky. The texture on the drawer edges was created with a chain saw. 38" high, 26" wide, 22" deep. *Photo, George Ensley*

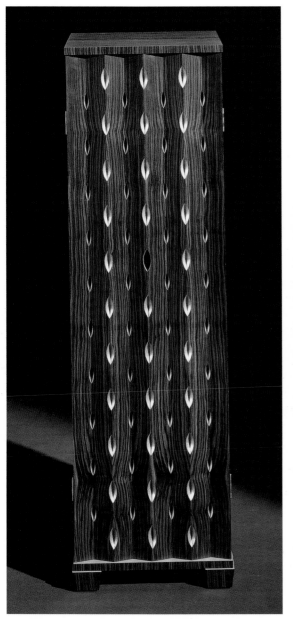

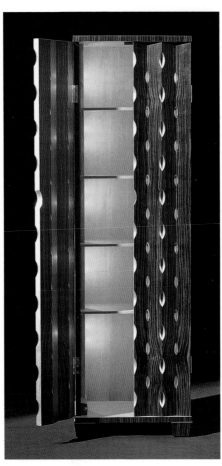

Far left:
Gregg Lipton. **Wizard Cabinet**. Closed. Macassar ebony, Swiss pear, and silver leaf. The interior is lit. 60" high, 18" wide, 13" deep. *Photo, Jeff Stevenson*

Left:
Gregg Lipton. **Wizard Cabinet**. Open. *Photo, Jeff Stevenson*

John Makepeace. **Eighteen**: Cabinet with 18 drawers. Burr elm and cherrywood. The structural cherry wood frame supports drawers of cherry veneered inside and out in burr elm, and cedar lined. Central rails in the drawer bottoms run on guides in the main frame. The drawers have bronze handles. The through dovetails are exposed to become a decorative feature at the corners (see detail).

John Makepeace. **Eighteen Cabinet**, detail. The swirling design in the burl and exquisite detailing illustrate the artist's ability to use the outstanding qualities of the wood advantageously. *Photo, Mike Murliss*

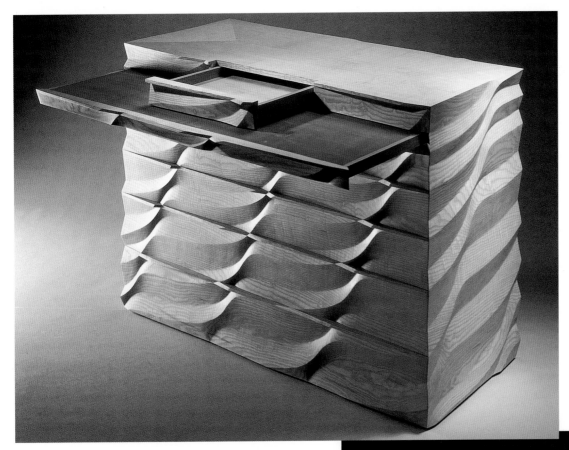

John Makepeace. **Desert Sand**. Chest of sculpted ripple ash. Ten drawers in chestnut and cedar. A suede covered pull-out shelf becomes the writing surface. The grain of this solid ripple ash runs continuously around each of the four sides. Using computer design techniques, the peaks and troughs spiral continuously around the form and coincide with the corners of the drawers, while the projection of the handles coincides with the troughs. The drawer interiors are made of oak and chestnut with scented cedar bottoms. *Photo, Mike Murliss*

John Makepeace. **Tuscan Obelisk**. Chest of drawers in English yew with carved lime wood and painted cypress trees. Obelisks, a feature of classical landscapes, were squared off tree trunks, and tapered like the tree itself. Rectilinear forms standing on the floor taper visually towards the ground, tending to look unstable. The obelisk responds to this phenomenon while providing a variety of drawer sizes. The external surface has been sculpted in response to the grain which runs continuously around the column. This adds to the tactile experience while overcoming the "techy's" temptation to produce perfectly flat surfaces which serve no purpose. The carved cypress trees complete the circle in time by referring to the origin of the obelisk. *Photo, Mike Murliss*

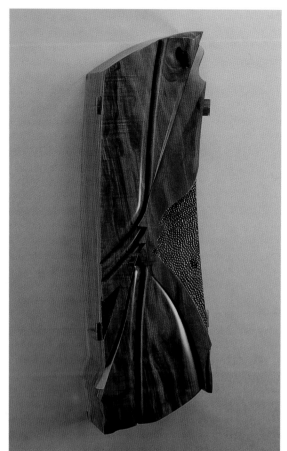

Charles B. Cobb. **Jewelry Case**, open.

Charles B. Cobb. **Wall-Hung Jewelry Case,** closed. Northern California walnut, maple, and bubinga. These began as doodles on paper and became a major creative problem because the doors had to open to accommodate the carving. 40" high, 13" wide, 12" deep. *Photo, Hap Sakwa*

Jefferson Shallenberger. **Art Cabinet #1,** closed. Redwood burl, pear, and holly. 56" high, 29" diam. *Courtesy, artist*

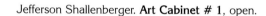

Jefferson Shallenberger. **Art Cabinet # 1,** open.

Michael Ireland. **Art's Mailbox**, open. As the top is lifted, the door slides forward. The fun of this piece was figuring out how to make the drawer delay mechanism open and close in time to miss the overhanging handle. He conjures the shape first and then feels the need to add a function. It's a case of "function following form." *Photo, artist*

Michael Ireland. **Art's Mailbox**, closed. An example of what Ireland calls his "discover function" series. When you open the object, its function is revealed. *Photo, artist*

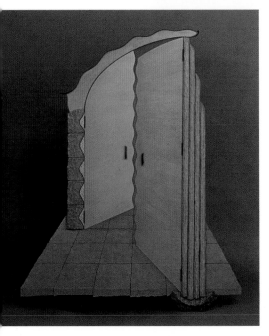

Jamie Robertson. **Media Cabinet**. Three-quarter view. The concept that a paradoxical flatness has depth tickles your curiosity – at first glance, it tells a lot but not enough. *Photo, artist*

Jamie Robertson. **Media Cabinet**, partially open. Carved mahogany, lime wood, purpleheart, curly African satinwood, dyed and tinted holly veneers, bending birch, and plywood substrates. The perspective is achieved by shapes of individual pieces, and the clever use of Japan colors, acrylic lacquer, and faux granite. 63" high, 51" wide, 24" deep. *Photo, artist*

Media Cabinet (left) by Jamie Robertson doesn't even hint that the viewer should expect the unexpected. Through the use of carefully placed lines and colors, there's a fascinating playfulness that mesmerizes the viewer to ponder over the *trompe l'oeil* image. They force the eye to move with the rhythms of the piece. He purposely skews the rules of perspective and slightly misaligns vanishing points. He places carved forms at visual termination points, balances hues, value, and saturation of each part, and uses an asymmetrical format. In some pieces, the wood is chosen with a dominant color and he explores its subtle grain variations to create an illusion of depth.

Mehmet Sahin Altug. **Tarsus Chest**. Hand painted chest with two doors and one drawer. 54" high, 22" wide, 15" deep. *Photo, Taylor Dabnay*

Mehmet Sahin Altug. **Bacchus Bar**. Three piece bar, shelf, and stool. Hand painted wood. Bar is 24" high, 38" wide 16" deep. The shelf is 48" high, 25" wide. 16" deep. The stool is 30" high, 12" diam. *Photo, Taylor Dabnay*

It's obvious that artist Mehmet Sahin Altug has a different perspective on what furniture should be. His *Cool Colors* sculptured furniture is carved and painted in vivid colors. The pieces are influenced by his Mediterranean childhood, and reflect Ancient Roman, Byzantine, and Middle Eastern architecture. Put one of these in any room and it can become an instant conversation piece, because each creation seems to have its own unique personality.

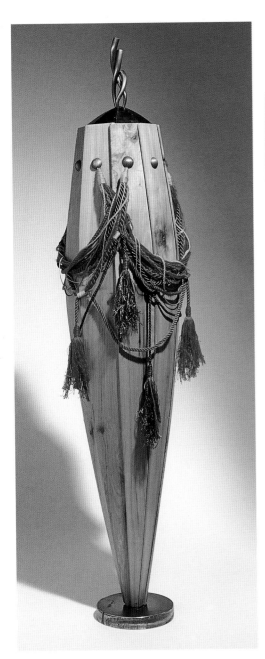

Chris Martin. **Pomp & Circumstance**. Hickory, steel, brass, mixed fibers, and beads. This reliquary or urn, was supposed to be pure sculpture but it ended up as a functional furnishing. It was constructed using the same techniques used by Viking boat builders. 48" high, 9" diam. *Photo, Bob Ebert*

Tommy Simpson. **She Was An Italain Evening.** Two-door armoire with five shelves. Basswood and acrylic paint. Simpson, a furniture maker with training as a painter, is strongly influenced by 20th century artists such as Wassily Kandinsky and Paul Klee. 79.5" high, 42" wide, 18" deep. *Courtesy , Leo Kaplan Modern Gallery, New York, New York*

105

Craig Nutt. **Nine Carrot Treasure Chest**. (Open)
Photo, John Lucas

Craig Nutt. **Nine Carrot Treasure Chest**. Walnut, curly maple, oil paint on carved wood. The legs are celery stalks. Looking like a carrot that has almost been pulled free of the earth, the exuberant exterior of this cabinet-on-chest belies its conservatively appointed interior of curly maple, walnut, brass, and glass. A "breadboard" that slides to the side just above the drawers provides support for examining treasures stored in the drawers. The center of the breadboard is a slice of carrot as though cut by a Vegomatic unit. 94" high, 20" wide, 20" deep. *Photo, John Lucas*

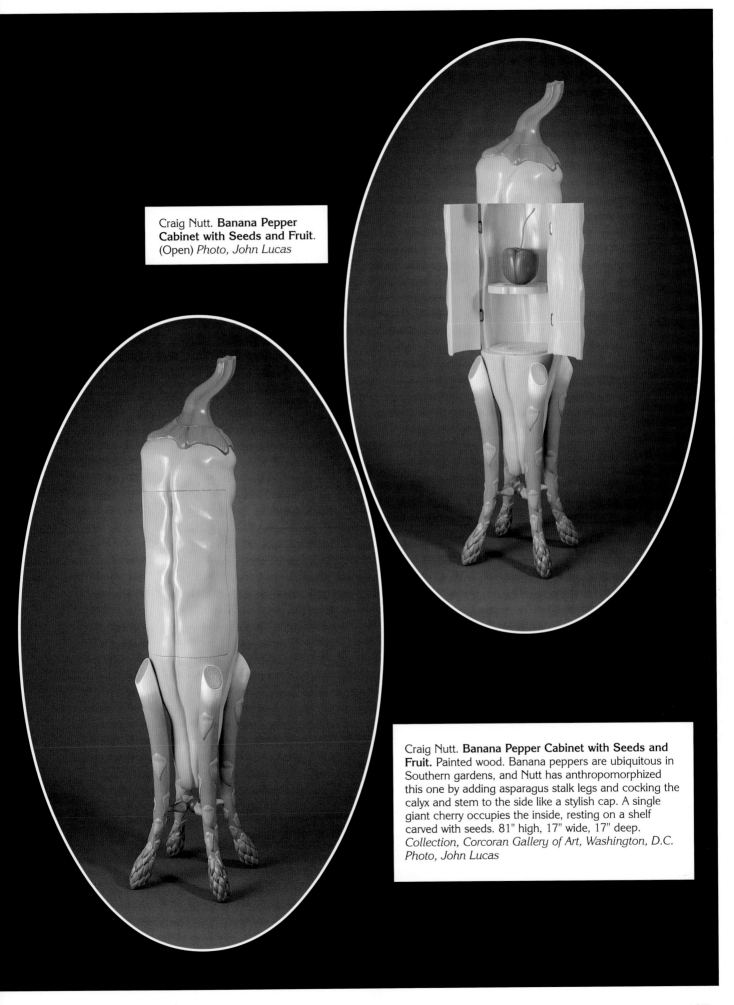

Craig Nutt. **Banana Pepper Cabinet with Seeds and Fruit.** (Open) *Photo, John Lucas*

Craig Nutt. **Banana Pepper Cabinet with Seeds and Fruit.** Painted wood. Banana peppers are ubiquitous in Southern gardens, and Nutt has anthropomorphized this one by adding asparagus stalk legs and cocking the calyx and stem to the side like a stylish cap. A single giant cherry occupies the inside, resting on a shelf carved with seeds. 81" high, 17" wide, 17" deep. *Collection, Corcoran Gallery of Art, Washington, D.C. Photo, John Lucas*

André Landry. **Hemmingway**. Clock cabinet. All mechanism parts are cherry wood, 90" high, 42" wide, 24" high. *Courtesy, artist*

Clocks and More

Banish the image of old grandfather clocks that have been relegated to collectibles. Bring in the new, the treasures of today and collectibles for the future. Start with the magnificently articulated hand made clocks from the studios of André Landry in Québec, Canada. These may be the ultimate example of someone with time on his hands because these pieces take time to create.

Landry's clock mechanisms, with each gear, each piece hand carved, are open to view so one can appreciate the beauty of the design, the precision, and complexity from all sides. Landry, after thirty years of working out his clock designs, has created ten models with different features. Some are made to stand on a mantel, others stand alone. They may inhabit beautiful cabinets that can serve as wine racks or cigar humidors. Each original design can be made in different woods and each is one of an edition of 200, signed and numbered. Making limited edition pieces is a valid practice for the studio furniture designer. It increases productivity and income without becoming a production shop. Each piece is still individually hand made by the artist.

Clocks also fascinate Rich Dunbrack. However, Landry's and Dunbrack's styles are diametrically opposed. Landry's clocks are hand-made precision instruments, beautiful, and serious. Dunbrack's clocks, constructed from found objects are pure imagination, fantasy. Created from the miscellaneous items of memories recycled into masterful works of art, they have a spark, a vitality, and assume human characteristics. Inevitably, people are amused and will smile or laugh when viewing them.

William McDowell's and Brent Skidmore's clocks fall midway between those by Landry and Dunbrack with innovative attributes that make them candidates for furniture art today.

Music stands, lamps, and sconces are projects that almost every wood artist tackles. Some make them as a part time endeavor as they learn to work with woods, tools, and ideas. Others make them when they are between other projects. A few continue to fashion them for specific clients or projects, or as a way of life. They don't abandon the art form; rather they continue to push it beyond any stylistic doldrums.

The same is true for specialty items such as a stand for a globe, a pedestal, clothes hooks, and cradles. In today's smaller homes, places to hang clothes need to be innovative and Kelli Kiyomi Kadokawa's whimsical painted coat and hat hooks would bring on a warming smile even coming in from an icy, snowy outdoors. Dennis Theisen's *Hall Tree Revisited*, is a modern adaptation of a traditional bit of old furniture. In addition to the seat, it has a bronze mirror, and argon mercury lights. That's very different from the bare light bulb with a pull chain on Grandfather's hall tree.

Lucky is the baby who basks in either of the award winning, wonderful cradles shown here by Dori Jenks and Ralph Kerr, and by Michael J. Brolly.

André Landry. **Clock on a Stand**. 93" high, 24" wide, 19" deep. Cherry wood mechanism. Available in maple, walnut, and mahogany. *Courtesy, artist*

André Landry. **Villion**. Wall clock. For use over a fireplace, or wall hung over a piece of furniture. Cherry mechanism, and available in mahogany, walnut or maple. 59" high, 38" wide, 15" deep. Courtesy, artist

Tommy Simpson. **Light Spot.** Basswood and acrylic paint. Sculpted and painted clock. Simpson concentrates on a narrative concept for a piece of furniture and the function is secondary. 77" high, 27" wide, 15.5" deep. *Courtesy, Leo Kaplan Modern Gallery, New York, New York*

111

Rick Dunbrack. **The Look-Out Post**. Clock. 8.5' high, 24" square. *Photo, Lori Anderson*

Rick Dunbrack. **Bella-Luna.** Clock. 7.5' high, 20" diameter at the base. *Photo, Lori Anderson*

Rick Dunbrack. **Pepperoni's Time Piece**. Grand Clock/Armoire. Fabricated from New England salvage, Victorian house fragments from New Hampshire, antique folk art carving, bronze doll's head, early American eel spear, clock dial from Prague, and a 110V geared clock movement. 9' high, 5' wide, 2' deep. *Photo, Lori Anderson*

Brent Skidmore. **Feathered Thoughts of the Passing Century.** Clock. Walnut, fiddleback makore, poplar, basswood, and acrylic paint. 80" high, 42" wide, 20" deep. *Photo, David Ramsey*

Brent Skidmore. **Shield over Mountain and Me**. Clock. Mahogany, poplar, pommele, sapele, basswood, walnut, aluminum, and steel. 98" high, 25" wide, 13" deep. *Photo, David Ramsey*

William McDowell. **Time Machine.** Cherry burl, African wenge, and maple. The sand doesn't move but the clock works. 20" high, 8" wide, 5" deep. *Photo, Gandino*

Garry Knox Bennett. **Table lamp #1**. Walnut, mahogany, brass, lamp parts, and 23k gold plate. The lamps are on swing arms so they can accommodate a chair placed at either side. 51.5" high, 16" wide, 35.5" deep. *Photo, M. Lee Fatheree*

Garry Knox Bennett. **Table lamp #2**. Wood, stainless steel, and acrylic. 65" high, 18" wide, 30" deep. Lamps are part of a series of 30 different styles. *Photo, M. Lee Fatheree*

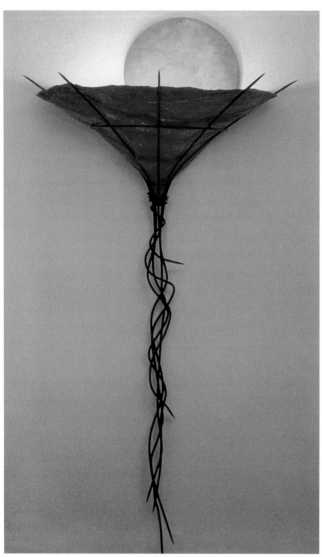

Derek Secor Davis. **Urban Flower Lamp**. Douglas fir, milk paint, and porcelain. Porcelain shade by Kate Inskeep. An industrial looking base is combined with an organic shade. 75" high, 9" wide, 9" deep. *Photo, Maddog Studio*

Chris Martin. **Setting Sun Sconce**. Steel, painted and gold leafed wood, and dyed rice paper. He says, "Using forged and twisted steel was a new approach that fostered a growth in my work." 88" high, 30" wide 18" deep. *Photo, artist*

Derek Secor Davis. **Double Flower Lamp IV.** Poplar, walnut, milk paint, and porcelain. Porcelain shade by Kate Inskeep. Based on organic forms. 78" high, 28" wide, 24" deep. *Photo, Maddog Studio*

116

Victor DiNovi. **Cherry Console with Vanity**. Mirror, XXIVV. 78"
high, 48" wide, 16" deep. *Photo, artist*

Victor DiNovi. **Marbled Top Table with Mirror.** Indonesian
rosewood. *Photo, artist*

Victor DiNovi's matching mirrors and consoles are gracefully elegant whether
the console stands on the floor or is wall hung. DiNovi's pieces nurture the needs of
the body and soul with objects of daily usefulness that are used, admired, respected,
and appreciated. He says, "Unfortunately, our culture gives too little attention to the
nature and effectiveness of artistic expression in the decorative arts. I believe in challenging people's assumptions about what furniture should look like and, by extension, challenging the essence of the way that they make any of life's assumptions."

Charles B. Cobb carries his odyssey of the unusual into mirror and console
shapes. As in his furniture, the mirrors, too, become captivating forms that are purely
sculptural and, almost incidentally, functional.

If a tree could grow a vanity table, it might look like Joël Urruty's example. Chris
Martin combines wood with other media, and Jamie Robertson applies his slanted
perspective and angles to a mirror with effects similar to his media cabinet, (page
99). If the mirror is a reflection of its maker, we can grasp an insight into the imagina-
tions of these talented artists.

Chris Martin. **Chamber Mirror**. This piece was inspired by a brooch that he had designed when he was making jewelry. He decided he was better able to work at a larger furniture scale than at a jewelry scale. *Photo, artist*

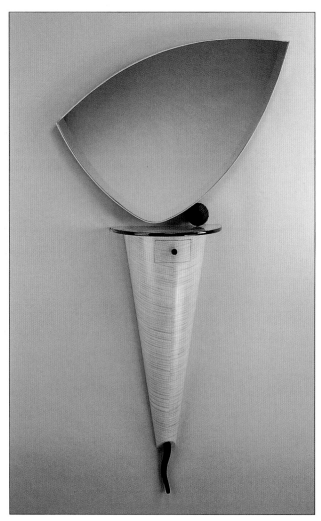

Charles B. Cobb. **Entry Table**. Medium Density Fiberboard, sepele veneer, 1/4" mirror, glass, molding paste, and paint. The leg is lathe turned. 72" high, 24" wide, 8" deep. *Photo, Hap Sakwa*

Chris Martin. **Mirror, Mirror**... Forged steel, white oak, and chain mail. The base was inspired by tribal tattoos. The wood was from used pallets laying behind his studio. He says, "Often some of the most beautiful pieces of wood I have ever used has been someone else's junk." 67" high, 52" wide, 21" deep. *Photo, artist*

Victor DiNovi. **Wall Mount Table with Drawer**. Imbuia. *Photo, artist*

Charles B. Cobb. **Entry Table**. Medium Density Fiberboard and curly maple veneer. 72" high, 24" wide, 8" deep. *Photo, Ron Bath*

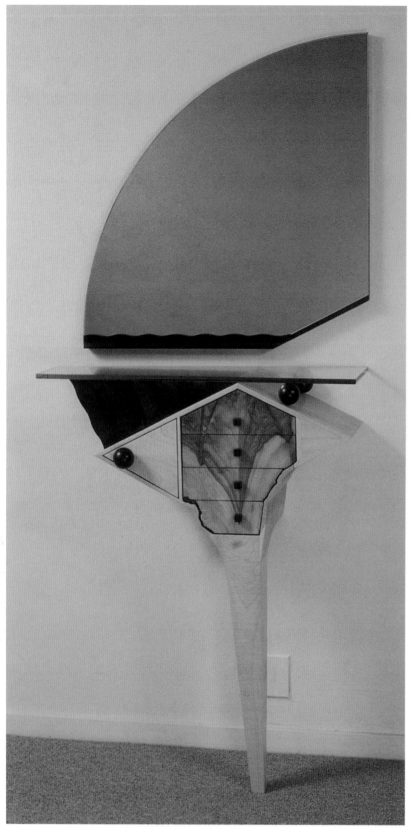

Charles B. Cobb. **Balancing Act**. Northern California walnut, maple, and African wenge. The drawer faces utilize an exquisite placement of the wood pattern. The knob is lathe turned. 72" high, 35" wide 12" deep.

Charles B. Cobb. **Abstract Mirror**. Purpleheart, 1/4" mirror, Medium Density Fiberboard, molding paste, and paint 36" high, 14" wide, 2" deep. *Photo, artist*

Jamie Robertson. **Courtship in the Maze**. Mirror. Carved mahogany, lime wood, laminated purpleheart, faux granite, Japan colors, and mirror. The skewed perspective and foreshortened elements mix with the mysterious animals and pull the viewer beyond his reflection, and into his imagination. 64" high, 48" wide, 3" deep. *Photo, artist*

Chris Martin. **War Club Mirror**. Walnut and cotton-wood burl, acrylic paint, and steel. Inspired by a Native American war club. The red pieces are dried strips of acrylic paint that are almost like plastic ribbons, and they are wrapped over steel rods. 33" high, 26" wide, 4" deep. *Photo, artist*

Merryll Saylan. **Tribute: Hans Coper**. Wood, paint, and dye. 54" high, 47" wide, 8" deep. Round bowls and vessels can be made in infinite sizes, shapes, and woods. Saylan explores a variety of iterations of a form inspired by the ceramics of Hans Coper, one of the most influential ceramicists of the 20th Century. *Photo, Hap Sakwa*

Chapter 3
Vessels, Bowls, and Turnings

Personally, the act of creation is as important as the object created. Each one gives me the confidence and wherewithal to do the next one, and the next one is always the best one.
Victor DiNovi

Suggest that someone picture a vessel or a bowl, and the usual mental image will be a container for holding something. Webster's dictionary concurs with that as a definition. However, the Webster committee may have to revise that definition for the future as today's artists reshape, rethink, and recreate vessel and bowl forms. An artist may begin with the image of a container in his head, but it may well end up as a sculptural form that may or may not function as a container. It might be more logical to think of its function as an object of beauty, designed by people who think passionately about the forms they create.

Ceramists have been dealing with the container concept for centuries. Ceramic vessels and ceramic shards have been unearthed from almost every ancient culture. Few wood artifacts remain because wood deteriorates over time. Ceramic vessels may have holes, negative shapes, protrusions, textures, and interesting surfaces that make them objects for pure esthetic enjoyment. Wood is moving in that direction, also.

Merryll Saylan takes her cue from work by a famous ceramist, and captures this concept in her *Tribute to Hans Coper*. His ceramics were so moving in their variety that she tackled a similar concept in a series of bowls exhibiting different shapes, proportions, woods, colors, sizes, and bases.

The capabilities of the lathe figures significantly in the creation of most shapes in this chapter. Of all the tools in the wood workers armamentarium, probably only the lathe generates objects dependent on, and characteristic of, what it can do. The lathe had been known and used since ancient Egypt, but in the 1970s, a new body of wood artists emerged. They became so imbued with the tool and its capabilities that they proudly assumed the status of "wood turners." They hoped that wood turning would become a separate craft division just as ceramics, textiles, metal, and others. Wood turner groups emerged throughout the country and continue still. Today, many devotees to the lathe have pushed its creative potential far beyond the traditional wood turned objects: the bowl, the plate, and the spindle.

They have used the lathe in combination with other tools, they have changed the relationship of the wood on the lathe's face plate to the turning spindles to create off-centered shapes. They have penetrated the vessel's walls with various tools so it no longer appears as a traditional container or vessel.

Today's artists are using the turned object as a jumping off point for fanciful figurative and organic sculptures. The vessel form may emerge as pure sculpture. It may even bypass the lathe and be carved with a chain saw.

Following are turned wood objects in an awesome variety of shapes. They flow from the exquisitely turned bowl form in exotic natural woods, to ingeniously shaped objects using today's tools so innovatively and brilliantly, that an entirely new chapter is being written in wood art.

Not only are surfaces penetrated, but inventive techniques have emerged for texturing, coloring, inlaying, and for combining like and unlike materials. The organic shaped vessel pioneered in the 1970s using imperfect woods and burls is still evident but mostly produced by hobbyists beginning to hone their skills. Many artists are using a variety of hand and power tools to purposely penetrate the walls

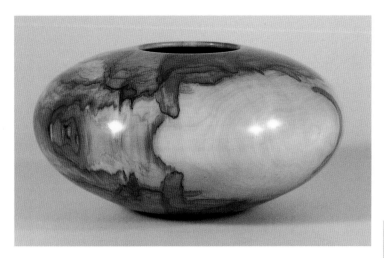

Philip Moulthrop. **Ash Leaf Maple Bowl**. The inherent beauty of the wood, its graining, the perfectly geometric shape, and a smooth, tactile surface, give this piece its aesthetic appeal. 8" high, 14" diam. *del Mano Gallery, Los Angeles, California. Courtesy, artist*

Philip Moulthrop. **Bundled Mosaic Bowl**. So called because sections of pine branches are set into the basic piece of wood that has been covered with epoxy. When it is dry, Moulthrop turns the piece to a final shape. He hollows the interior and smoothes the exterior to result in a mosaic bowl of natural wood against a stark black background. 8" high, 8.5" diam. *del Mano Gallery, Los Angeles, California. Courtesy, artist*

of the vessels, and to deconstruct the forms and assemble them in new relationships. Turners who are bypassing the lathe and carving directly into a block with other tools are developing forms that may be reminiscent of their turning backgrounds.

Still, many turners remain pure turners loyal to the lathe. Philip Moulthrop says, "I create pieces using simple turned shapes and forms that will best display the colors and patterns inherent in the wood. My use of smooth curving surfaces and lack of carvings or other embellishments, is intended to better display the wood and not compete with it."

Yet Moulthrop's techniques go beyond the vessel simply turned from a wood block. He may begin with a spheroid form, but then he alters the visual impact of the piece. He mixes epoxy with sawdust and covers the blank surface with it. Next, he sets cross sections of pine branches into the epoxy and lets it dry. Only then does he turn the piece to shape, hollowing the interior, and sanding the outside to bring out the pattern. The result is a pattern of light wood against the dark background of the bowl.

Bob Stocksdale, in his most productive years, used only a few tools to make bowls that are elegant in their simplicity and in the way they exploit the wood's natural grains and colors. A retrospective show of Stocksdale's bowls at the Mingea Museum in San Diego, California, in 2002, made each vessel appear as a precious jewel in its display case. It was like a symphony of grains and textures playing similar notes but each with a special vibrancy. Stocksdale has noted that his practice of using only a few tools allowed him to spend more time creating rather than sharpening blades.

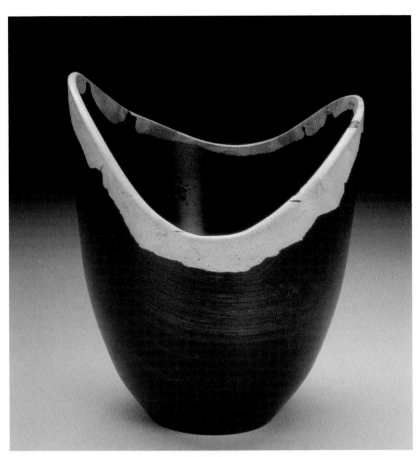

Bob Stocksdale. **Untitled Bowl**. Mpingo wood. Stocksdale favored exotic woods with unique grains and natural features he could exploit to create his exquisite bowls. He used only basic tools and simple forms. 6" high, 5" diam. *del Mano Gallery, Los Angeles, California. Photo, David Peters.*

Bob Stocksdale. **Canalete Bowl**. A heavily grained bowl of Mexican wood, with thick walls and a round shape. Many of his bowls are more oval, but the shape is often determined by the unique characteristics in the wood. 5" high, 6.5" diam. *del Mano Gallery, Los Angeles, California. Photo, David Peters.*

Ron Kent. **Translucent Vessel**. Norfolk pine, indigenous to Kent's home in Hawaii, became his material of choice when he discovered its unique knot patterns, and dramatic spalting. By soaking the wood in vats of oil, he is able to turn the wood very thin, and create wide and flared forms resting on small bases. 12" high, 16" diam. Photo, artist

Ron Kent. **Translucent Vessel**. Norfolk pine. Achieving evenly thin vessel walls graduating from a wide top to a small base is a characteristic of Kent's translucent bowls. 10" high, 8" diam. *Photo, artist*

Ron Kent exploits the nature of Norfolk pine wood for turning nearly paper thin bowls that appear translucent when held up to the light. He began turning bowls as a hobby, and was so successful that he became a full time craftsman after retiring from his career as a stockbroker in Hawaii. His unique bowls are in prestigious collections including the Renwick Gallery of the Smithsonian Institution, Washington D.C., the Metropolitan Museum of Art, New York, New York, and the Louvre, Paris, France.

Ron Kent is among several of today's wood artists whose work appeared in my earlier book, *Creating Small Wood Objects as Functional Sculpture,* published in 1976. In revisiting artists for this book it was particularly gratifying to see how their work had changed, matured, and been accepted by the public.

I had casually met William Hunter in 1976 at a tourist Trading Post in El Portal, California, where I photographed his manzanita burl weed vases. Today, his turnings are style setters. They are light years beyond his early pieces in concept and technique. His vessels, and the sculptures that evolved by deconstructing the turned forms and restructuring the pieces into knotted and helical forms, have set the idea of lathe work onto a new path that is influencing other artists.

Hunter's *Basket Series* shows an interplay between interior and surface, front and back, top and bottom, positive and negative, light and shadow, and they dance between reality and illusion. Patterns and their relationships assume a continuously shifting, morphing life as the viewer moves around the piece. A tension arises between what is perceived and what is thought to be true.

Frank E. Cummings III, as a young art instructor at a California University, had just returned from studying the crafts in Africa in 1976 when I first interviewed him. He had translated images he had found there into unique jewelry and small vessels. Today his exquisitely crafted vessels with hand carved exotic woods, gold, and other precious components combine to make an incredibly beautiful statement.

Several artists who contacted me for this book told me that an earlier book had directed and molded their careers as wood turners. Terry Martin, among today's prolific and respected wood artists, said *Small Wood Objects as Functional Sculpture* was a catalyst and turning point in his life (no pun intended) and set him on a

Leon Lacoursiere. **Bowl**. Bird's eye maple, carved, and painted. The bowl takes advantage of the wood pattern for its texture. The swirling lines are carved and the edges are highlighted with paint. 5" high 7" diam. *del Mano Gallery, Los Angeles, California. Photo, David Peters*

David Ellsworth. Left: **Pot**. Hickory burl. 7" high, 3" diam. Right **Black Pot-Dawn**. Ash. *Photo, artist*

career that has earned him star status in the field. He, too, has developed directions for the turned object that took it from the vessel form into pure sculpture.

In addition to the resourcefulness of the artists, and the ingenious forms that have evolved, other changes and trends may be noted. Primarily, the simple salad bowl style can no longer find its way to the professional art milieu on the basis that it is handmade. Such turned bowls are more often the work of hobbyists, production wood manufacturers, and importers.

Heavily laminated woods, turned into bowls, have lost some of their popularity. Because wood is a natural medium and tends to shrink and swell, the glues used in the laminates often separate over time. Many artists are working with "green wood" rather than seasoned and cured wood. Green wood is easier to turn because it is softer; the pores still retain water. But after it is turned it may distort. Often that unexpected distortion will enhance a form and tell the story of the wood. Alternately, it may fracture or crack and the object may be a disaster.

Some artists strive for more color in their bowls than one or two woods will produce. They may combine woods with inherent complimentary or contrasting colors. They may "enhance" the piece by any number of ingenious colorants. Paint, of course, is the most obvious. Artists such as Binh Pho and Ron Fleming tend to use the form as a canvas for airbrushing rather than painting with a brush or spray. Ed Zbik adds inlays into his bowls, emulating the work of Native Americans. Merryll Saylan uses fiber-reactive dyes.

The stories the artists tell about their inspirations, methods, and approaches are many, and gratifying, and some accompany their pieces. The results are awesome and sure to astound those who are unfamiliar with, or haven't kept up with the field. Their experiences, philosophies, and thought processes may inspire those who are staunch supporters of lathe work to try a new approach, or to venture beyond that tool and strive for inventive, creative shapes, and forms with companion tools. Expanded comments often may be found on an individual artist's Web site. They should be considered an extension of the copy found here and an essential tool of today's wood turner and researcher.

The Role of the Lathe

Most vessels shown in this chapter owe their being to the use of the lathe, a woodworking power tool. The lathe's principle function is to rotate a piece of wood on its protruding spindle so that a wood worker, using a sharp bladed tool, can shape the piece of wood in the round as the lathe spins. Some tools are made exclusively for hollowing out the inside of the vessel. In the following series John Jordan demonstrates how a bowl results from the interaction of the artist's chisel blade on the spinning piece of wood. Initially, shapes were made by keeping the wood only on the one axis of the spindle. With experimentation, artists began changing the relation of the wood to the faceplate that secures it so that different angles could be accomplished.

The woods used might be blocks of cut lumber, slices of board laminated to make up the rough shape, or a burl. Boards and lumber from the straight part of a tree trunk have grain, and that grain can differ depending on the tree's growth pattern, where it was on the tree, and how the wood has been sawn.

A burl may consist of a gnarly cluster of small stalks growing within the form. The burl has grain that swirls in many directions because of its erratic growth. Burls yield interesting designs, textures, and colors. They are unpredictable for carving; the erratic graining can make carving difficult with conventional carving tools. However, because the grain is not straight, there is less chance of splitting the wood along natural grain lines that exist in a dressed piece of lumber.

Spalted wood, mentioned in Chapter 1, deserves mention again. Because spalted wood is consistently inconsistent in appearance, it is in high demand within the decorative wood market. Each piece is unique and completely different from the next. One tree may have good workable spalted wood, while the next, although appearing similar, may be useless. Only by working with spalted wood can one gain the knowledge necessary to succeed with, and fully appreciate, the challenges of this unpredictable material.

Artist woodworkers tend to experiment and push the potential of available equipment to create what they can imagine. They inventively overcome the supposed limits of a tool and make it work to accomplish their ends.

That's part of the creativity, too. Most woodworkers will share this knowledge in writings and during meetings with other woodworkers.

John Jordan. **White House Jar**. Turned, carved, and dyed box elder with a fossil ivory detail at the top. 13" high, 9" diam. Collection, White House, Washington, D.C. *Photo, John S. Cummings.*

Stephen Gleasner. **Lost Words**. Birch and maple. The organic spacing of the carving strokes interrupt the layering of the laminations so that rippled water is suggested. The colors play on an ocean theme, with the blue of the surface dropping away into darkness. The inside is not textured; instead, it is colored brilliant yellow to contrast with the darker world below and on the outside surface. 13" high, 7" diam. *del Mano Gallery, Los Angeles, California. Photo, Bill Gleasner*

Stephen Gleasner. **Pewter Rising**. Birch and rosewood. This piece uses a measured layout to determine the location of coves. The carving here is more ordered than in "Lost Words." They share a similar tension between the textured outside of the vessel and its uninterrupted interior. 11" high. 8" diam. *del Mano Gallery, Los Angeles, California. Photo, Bill Gleasner*

Michael Bauermeister. **Sprouts**. A group of several vessels in various woods. These pieces are laminated from up to 30 tapered layers of wood. The wedge-shaped tapers are what give each piece its lively, twisting shape. The pieces vary from 18" to 40" tall. *Photo, artist*

Jack R. Slentz. **Distortion**. A Group of Individuals. Cherry, ash, and red oak. Artists use a variety of personal visual concepts for ideas. 40" high, 33" wide, 18" deep. Permanent collection of the Renwick Gallery of the Smithsonian Institution, Washington, D.C. *Photo, Sean Moorman*

Jack Slentz reduces and simplifies natural and man-made forms. His points of departure may be manhole covers, trees, seedpods, spears, shields, masks, and primitive tools and utensils. Influenced by their forms, patterns, and textures, he incorporates a sense of rhythm that implies movement. He believes strongly in showing the mark of the tool in the finished work.

John Jordan. **Lidded Vessel**. Box elder. Carefully placed ridges, natural imperfections, and coloration in the wood are combined for interesting surface treatments. 8" high, 7.5" diam. *Photo, artist*

Marcus Tatton. **Shard II**. Tasmanian Blackwood. Originally carved as a full round vessel it is now a wall sculpture. The repeat circles and dashes suggest digital information, molecular structure, and anthropomorphic levels of our perceptions. The universal law of dissipation is its inspiration. *del Mano Gallery, Los Angeles, California. Photo, David Peters*

Jack R. Slentz. **Swirling Vessel**. Jarrah burl and hickory. Slentz' pieces often look crude and primitive but that's on purpose. He says, "It's a beauty that comes from the purity and simplicity of form that is emphasized by showing the mark of the tool." 50" high, 23" wide, 21" deep. *Photo, Sean Moorman*

James Christiansen. **Nakisha's Box**. Maple burl and ebony. The root form as a part of a box design portrays the origin of wood as growing from the earth. 2" high, 6" diam. *Photo, Will Simpson*

141

Mike Scott. **Fluted Form**. Oak burl, sandblasted and bleached. 6" high, 11" diam. *del Mano Gallery, Los Angeles, California. Photo, Tony Boase*

Jacques Vesery. **I Wish I Knew What I Know Now**. Textured and burned cherry with maple rim, and a carved and textured boxwood egg. Vesery says, "After carving the egg, it needed a base to set it off and a nest seemed the appropriate addition. Little did I realize the nest would become the focus, and a new texture in my work would be hatched." Collection, Ed and Rasa Knudsen. 2" high, 11" diam. *Photo, Robert Diamante*

Kip Christensen. **Whited Sepulcher Series 011**. Linden bass burl. The title, Whited Sepulcher, is taken from a reference in the New Testament, Matthew Chapter. The textural treatments give the sense and feeling of a weather worn surface with sections that have been recently smoothed and polished to de-emphasize the decomposition and erosion over time. 7" high, 9" wide. *Photo, Photocraft*

Kip Christensen. **Lidded Jewelry Bowl**. Elk antler, coral, ebony, and pink ivory wood. Nature has created antler to be both resilient and elegant. Remarkably, male elk produce a new set of antlers each year. The result is that antler is the fastest growing bony structure found in the animal kingdom. 2.25" high, 3.75" diam. *Photo, Photocraft*

Frank E. Cummings III. **Embrace**. Created from a single piece of African Blackwood. Inlays of tagua nut and 18k gold. Cummings opened up the sides of his sculptural vessels by hand carving linear elements to enclose space within the sides of the form. 9.75" high, 4.5" diam. *Photo, artist*

Pierced Pieces

As artists deviate from the traditional shapes and techniques for creating wood art, a variety of changes appear. Walls had been solid to conform to the necessity for holding or containing something. Then artists began penetrating the surfaces. In the book, *Wood Turning In North American Since 1930,* published in 2001 by The Wood Turning Center, only a few examples illustrate negative shapes in the pieces, and these are essentially the result of natural imperfections in the wood such as knot holes, cracks, or fissures.

Purposely planned negative shapes begin to appear in vessels in the late 1990s and the practice is apparent in the work by Frank E. Cummings III, Peter Hromek, Ben Trupperbäumer, and William Hunter. Art Liestman's jig saw puzzle-like vessels fall into that category, also. After that, the pierced wall seems to have led to a breaking down of the wall entirely. The resulting shapes become sculpture as seen in Chapter 4. Thus, the line between vessel and sculpture has been blurred.

Frank E. Cummings III. **Carousel—Age of Awareness**. Walnut with black onyx stones, and 18k gold. He carried the idea of opening the sides of the vessel further in this incredibly detailed and ambitious vessel. The hand carved loops at the top simulate tatted lace-like elements. Hand carved black ebony horses strut proudly between uprights set with precious stones. Cummings, a virtuoso of wood and jewelry techniques, enjoys a well-deserved international reputation. 16.5" tall, 12" diam. *Photo, artist*

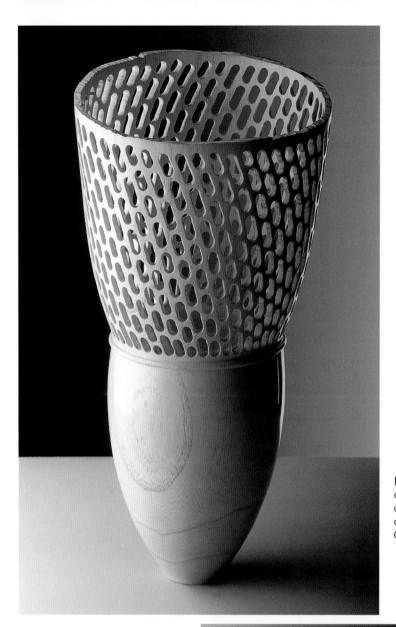

Peter Hromek. **Ash vessel**. Hromek also penetrates the walls of the vessel. The combination of unique form and the repeat of negative spaces combine to provide texture and an interplay of light and shadow. 10" high, 14" diam. *Photo, Georg Gottbrath*

Peter Hromek. **Ash Vessel**. The open form with edges that dip and surge balances on a small rounded base that defies the ability to balance, but it does. 12.5" high, 7" diam. *Photo, Georg Gottbrath*

Marcus Tatton. **Home of the Ringtail**. Black-heart sassafras. Pierced rim. The ringtail possum is endemic to Tasmania. Here it is carved life size, snuffling into its hollow tree home. Ringtail possums are an indicator of the health of a forest as they prefer to live high in the old hollows of ancient trees. 23" high, 18" diam. *del Mano Gallery, Los Angeles, California. Photo, David Peters*

Ben Trupperbäumer. **Platter.** The artist carves his work, no lathe is used. But the concept is a flat vessel form that could have been lathe turned, then areas opened up for negative shapes. *Courtesy, del Mano Gallery, Los Angeles, California. Photo, David Peters*

William Hunter. **Kinetic Rhythms**. Cocobolo. 8" high, 11.75" diam. Hunter explains, "The motive for Kinetic Rhythms was to sculpt and define relationships between volume and space, form and line, light and shadow, interior and exterior, movement and rest. At times I felt as if I was working on the delicate skeletal structure of the vessel." Collection, The Mint Museum, Charlottesville, North Carolina. *Photo, Hap Sakwa*

William Hunter. **Retusa Basket**. Cocobolo. Hunter's objective is to energize a vessel by sculpting and cutting it to add to its narrative. This piece explores lyrical movement, fluidity, and exchanging static for dynamic values. 5.75" high, 10.5" diam. Collection, The Mint Museum, Charlottesville, North Carolina. *Photo, George Post*

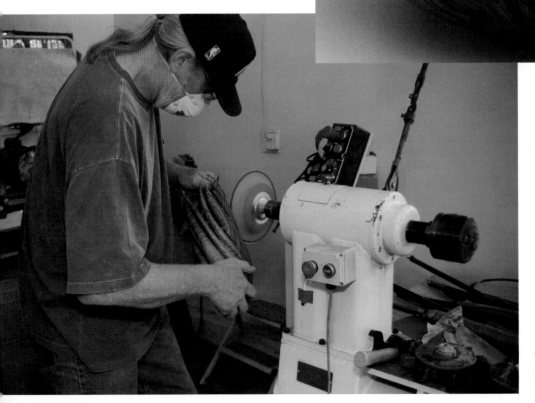

William Hunter uses a disk sander to sculpt the wood, cutting through a turned shape to open it up.

William Hunter. **Aphrodite.** Cocobolo. The idea was to add a feeling of gesture to a spiral. 13.75" high, 6.5" diam. *Photo, Hap Sakwa*

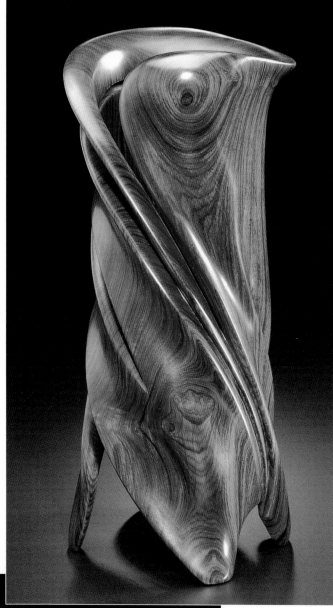

William Hunter. **Vallarta Shores**. Cocobolo. Deconstructing vessels results in a visual complexity and a compounding of inter-relationships and perspectives. 5" high, 10" diam. (2 pieces). *Photo, Hap Sakwa*

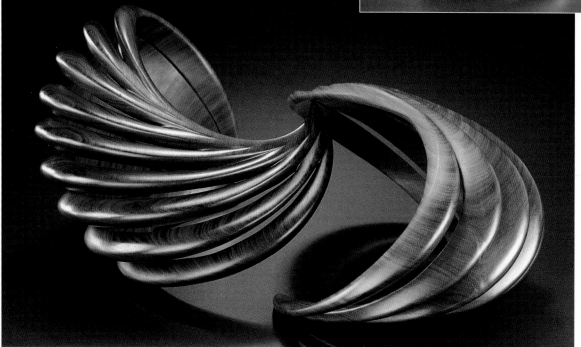

Art Liestman. **Mostly**. Big leaf maple and ebony. 5" tall, 4.75" diam.
Photo, Kenji Nagai

Art Liestman. Left to right: **Gratitude, Over the Fields, Change of Plan**. Big leaf maple and ebony.
Gratitude: 4.75" high, 4.74" diam. Over the Fields: 9.25" high, 5.25" diam. Change of Plan 4.2"
high, 4" diam. *Photo, Kenji Nagai*

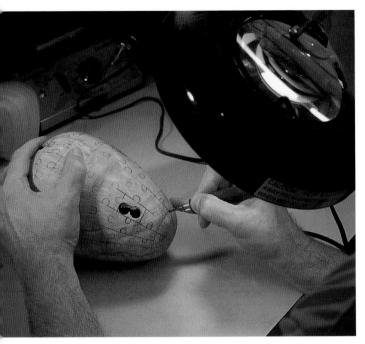

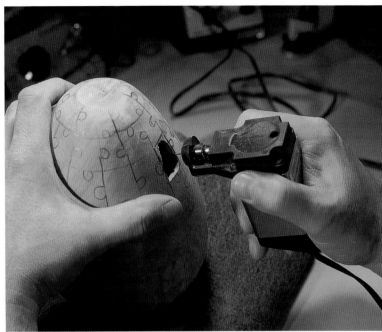

Art Liestman burns the puzzle outlines with a pyrography tool. *Photo, Kenji Nagai*

He removes a piece with a miniature jig saw. *Photo, Kenji Nagai*

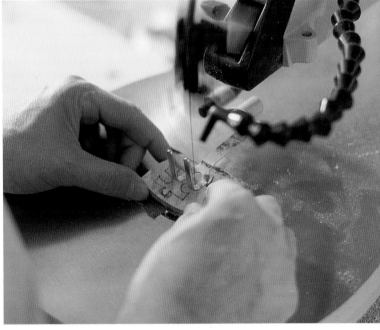

He cleans the edge of a removed piece with a rotary carving tool. *Photo, Kenji Nagai*

Art Liestman cuts a "loose" piece from a turned piece of the same wood. The loose pieces are purposely not the shape that would fit in the space though they appear as if they would. *Photo, Kenji Nagai*

Surface Carving

In viewing and studying the carved images on the vessels, consider that many designs and effects are not surface decorations for the sake of decorating. Most have much thought and significance to them. Michelle Holzapfel's range of carving ideas is infinite and based on her various interests. Often her pieces represent literary symbolism or references to music. Her early training was in fiber arts, so many of her pieces contain woven and knotted forms. Clay Foster's fonts are replete with symbolism that relate to his view of life. The font with the snake around it states the approach to, or avoidance, that many people feel about snakes. To Foster, they embody many of life's characteristics.

Ron Fleming's friendly looking dragons are a throwback to his attitude about dragons from childhood storybooks. But he also takes many of his ideas from nature, carving flowers and a variety of plant forms.

Michelle Holzapfel. **Elemental Vase.** Cherry burl. 7" high, 15" diam. *Photo, David Holzapfel*

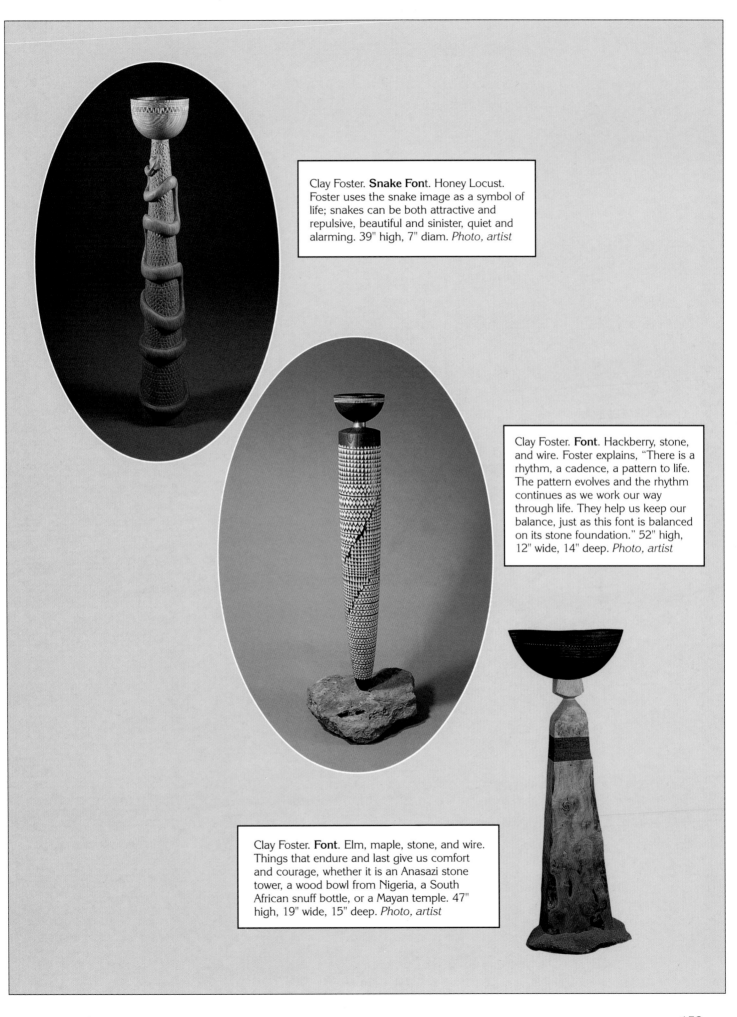

Clay Foster. **Snake Font**. Honey Locust.
Foster uses the snake image as a symbol of
life; snakes can be both attractive and
repulsive, beautiful and sinister, quiet and
alarming. 39" high, 7" diam. *Photo, artist*

Clay Foster. **Font**. Hackberry, stone,
and wire. Foster explains, "There is a
rhythm, a cadence, a pattern to life.
The pattern evolves and the rhythm
continues as we work our way
through life. They help us keep our
balance, just as this font is balanced
on its stone foundation." 52" high,
12" wide, 14" deep. *Photo, artist*

Clay Foster. **Font**. Elm, maple, stone, and wire.
Things that endure and last give us comfort
and courage, whether it is an Anasazi stone
tower, a wood bowl from Nigeria, a South
African snuff bottle, or a Mayan temple. 47"
high, 19" wide, 15" deep. *Photo, artist*

Ron Fleming. **Fishhook**. Spalted hackberry and Osage orange. A stylized impression of a cactus. The spalting lines of the wood yield the texture of the cactus. Toothpicks that have been steamed, bent, and sanded to points replicate the spines on the cactus. *Photo, Bob Hawks*

Jacques Vesery. **Washing the Shadows from My Pillow**. Carved cherry, with amboyna burl, and 23.5k gold leaf. Dreams are often his inspiration, whether they are daydreams, or those in the quiet of night. 4" diam. Collection, Dr. Minda Gold. *Photo, Robert Diamante*

Jacques Vesery. **Friends of a Feather**. Carved cherry and boxwood eggs are made in various sizes. They are akin to turning a bowl inside out. *Photo, Robert Diamante*

Ron Fleming. **Ling Chih**. Tulip poplar. The form is based on a tree fungus. Ling Chih is the name of a candy made from a mushroom by the Chinese. 17" high, 15" diam. *Photo, artist*

Ron Fleming. Inspiration for **Ling Chih**. *Photo, artist*

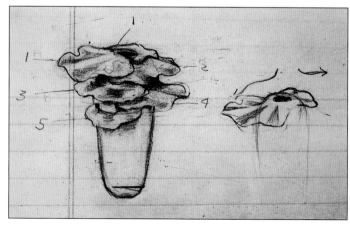

Drawing of the fungus. *Photo, artist*

Ron Fleming. **Andora**. Mahogany. Inspired by a fern that grows in East Africa. 15.5" high, 13" deep. *Photo, artist*

Ron Fleming. **Dragon Dance**. Redwood burl. Fairytale dragons fascinated Fleming as a child. He tried to create a piece where the dragons were kind, gentle, playful, loving, and caring, not fierce nor cartoon-like characters. He wanted them to just be fun. Eight different intertwined dragon images dance and romp around the vessel on a bed of ocean waves. 15" high, 19" diam. *Photo, Bob Hawks*

Ron Fleming. **Dragon Dance**. Close-up of the carving details. *Photo, Bob Hawks*

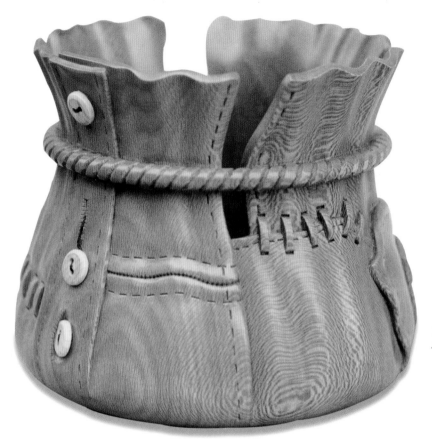

Nikolai Ossipov. **Fabric Bowl**. Bowl turned and carved of one piece of sycamore. 5.25" high, 6.75" diam. *del Mano Gallery, Los Angeles, California.. Photo, artist*

Johannes Michaelson and Steve Loar. **New This Season**. Maple Hats. Two styles from many available in different woods and in three sizes. The artists have these in many collections. *del Mano Gallery, Los Angeles, California. Photo, artists*

Christian Burchard. **Tightlaced**. Madrona burl. The forms give a glimpse of possibilities or act as metaphors serving as a transport for ideas. Some are solely because they were fun to make. *Photo, artist*

Christian Burchard. **Baskets**. Madrona burl. Hand carved from green wood. These forms change as they dry. From 15" to 16" high. *Photo, artist*

The madrona wood used by Christian Burchard grows wild along the northwest United States coast and has a wide range of colors and textures. It resists all attempts to dry evenly, warping or cracking and hardening as it dries. Burchard turns it while green and is easy to cut and handle. He takes advantage of the warping as the wood dries to create attitude, gesture, and, when grouped together, relationships. The soft surface texture is achieved by using the cutting edge of his tools and light sandblasting. Most openings are slightly burnt for contrast and to enhance their looseness. When the pieces are turned very thin, they don't crack but when the wood is left thick, the cracking can create a very dramatic effect. Sometimes he bleaches the wood to lighten it. His pieces often tell stories; some exist only because they were fun to make.

Peter Hromek. **Three-legged vessel**. Maple. Hromek's vessels are mainly inspired by plants, flowers, seed capules, and such. This work was made in three separate parts, and assembled. Hromek says the beauty and uniqueness of wood motivate him to find and create a form that combines perfection and harmony. Each time he creates a piece, the process consists of curiosity, ingeniousness, experimentation, and searching. In time, the beauty of the wood becomes less significant and the object's form becomes the most important aspect of the creation process. 17" high. *Photo, Georg Gossbrath*

Peter Hromek. **Pear Tree Turning**. Pear wood. Lathe turned and further worked by hand. Peter Hromek also opens up the vessel's sides. 8" high, 13" wide. *Photo, Georg Gossbrath*

Mark Sfirri. **Gessoed French Vessels.** Poplar and paint. Many of these seemingly
"wacky" shapes are the result of off-center turning. From 2" to 13" high. *Photo, artist*

Niel Stoutenburg. **Unicellular Vessels**. Various wood; curly maple, ash, poplar, quilted maple, black palm wood, boxwood, and African black wood. The forms are inspired by nature's microscopic world (unicellular creatures), the sea world, insect world, the simple graceful lines of a sculpted body, and the limitless texture variations. They are hollow, turned to a very thin wall through a small opening. The tails are carved. 2" to 3" diam. Collection, Edward Merrin Gallery. *Photo, Kevin Hogarth*

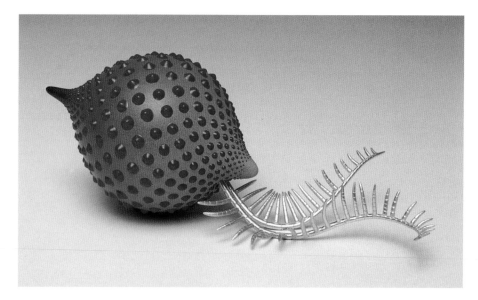

Louise Hibbert. **Sea Creature**. Hibbert focuses on different creatures from marine life and they are the forms that inspire her work. del Mano Gallery, Los Angeles, California. *Photo, David Peters*

Matthew Hill. **Lidded Box.** Maple and ebony. Hill likes to work in wood because it is amazingly strong in relation to its weight, is able to take fine detail, and malleable enough to be shaped with hand tools. 4" high, 6" wide, 6" deep. *del Mano Gallery, Los Angeles, California. Photo, David Peters*

Michael Bauermeister. Vessels on display show the range of sizes, forms, and colors the artist has conceived. For these pieces concentric rings are cut from a wide board and laminated to form the rough shape that is then carved, and/or turned to final form, and sanded. Tool marks may be left visible or sometimes smoothed off completely. Various finishes and surface treatments are used. The tall vessels have an almost human, figural presence. *Courtesy, artist*

Michael Bauermeister. **Color Mixing Vessel**. Poplar, painted and turned. Painting was done on the piece as it rotated on the lathe. The result is not visible until the lathe is turned off. Caution, this technique may induce dizziness. 42" high, 16" diam. *Photo, artist*

Michael Bauermeister says, " I have chosen the wood vessel for my sculptural ideas because I find it to be a comfortable place for both the viewer and myself to start. From here I can explore the issues of form, texture, scale and color, all in the natural beauty of wood."

Bauermeister's work involves a variety of finishes and surface treatments. The resulting object has an ambiguous appeal. New, yet primitive; organic, but man made. Even the material is difficult to identify. Sculptures have a dynamic shape, repeat grain patterns, and are surprisingly lightweight.

163

Color Surfaces

Many artists exploit the natural colors of woods. But often an artist wants to enhance the tones, or they want more color so they dip into palettes from other media such as paint, rubbing tones into the wood, using dyes, inlays, and whatever they can make work for the effects they want. Some may use more than one medium. Scorching and burning, and other techniques are used extensively, but carefully. Color is also introduced by combining other media with the wood, such as horn, metals, brass and iron, even inlaying natural stones, gold, and so forth. These materials also appear in sculpture and objects.

Simon Levy says, "It's the hollow vessel form that attracts me to woodturning. The contained space hidden inside is silent, suspended, and mysterious – the unknown. The exterior is where each piece finds its individuality and begins to tell its own story. Wood is an inviting material to embellish and patterns emerge that add movement, dimension, and texture to the already visible wood grain. My surfaces are engraved, carved, wood burned, stamped, drawn upon and painted. Variations can be sparse and bold or complex and subtle. The goal is to make a piece of art that continues to speak to the viewer."

Ron Fleming. **Datura**. Basswood and acrylic. Inspired by Jimson weed that grows in their garden. 13.5" high, 17" deep. *Photo, Bob Hawks*

Ron and Patti Fleming. **Yama Yuri**, "Mountain Lily" in Chinese. Basswood and acrylic. 36" high, 17" deep.
Designed by Patti Fleming, turned and painted by Ron Fleming. Process photos follow. *Photo, Bob Hawks*

A drawing establishes the concept for the vase and the placement of the design.

The natural flower lily, "yama yuri," that inspired the design. The lilies are painted in airbrush at full size. The vase's interior is finished in a deep green, high gloss lacquer to contrast with the matte exterior.

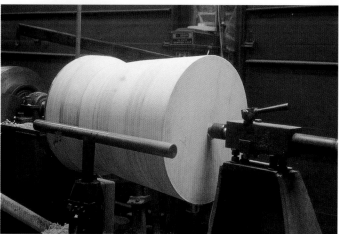

The basswood segments are glued up.

Ron starts to turn the wood on the lathe. First he hollows out the inside, and then shapes the outside as the wood turns on the lathe.

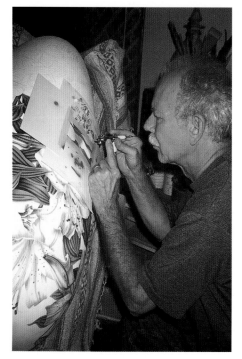

After the wood has been sanded and primed, the floral pattern is painted with an airbrush.

Close up of the final decoration. Each painted lily is the actual size of the real flower. *Photo series, Bob Hawks*

Binh Pho's beautifully painted turned vessels from his *Warrior Series* were inspired by the art of Chinese face painting. Ancient mask painting developed by Wu-Hsiang Dee in the Song dynasty originally inspired this unique art form. The painted masks were used in the battlefield to represent dreadful figures that would frighten the enemy. Eventually, the masks were employed in the opera and theatre, and to indicate a character's social standing and personality.

Later, because it was difficult to wear masks and inconvenient to manufacture them, colors were painted directly on the actors faces. An unpainted face represented a faithful and nice person. A multi-color face represented a wicked person, a red face was for someone who was loyal and straight; a black face was for characters who were brave and had perseverance. Buffoons were painted with colored spots. These conventions are still practiced in modern theatre.

Binh Pho has cleverly combined his turned sculpture pieces with piercing and airbrushing techniques to bring back the images of these ancient warriors.

Binh Pho. **Dynasty.** Turned, pierced, and airbrushed with transparent acrylic paint. 15" high 10" diam. *Photo, artist*

Binh Pho. **Warrior #2**. Turned, pierced, and airbrushed with transparent acrylic paint. 18" high 8" diam. *Photo, artist*

Binh Pho. **Warrior #1**. Turned, pierced, and airbrushed with transparent acrylic paint. 12" high, 8" diam. *Photo, artist*

Binh Pho. **Zen**. Turned, pierced, and airbrushed with transparent acrylic paint. The textured surface is contrasted with the smooth surface of the colors. The piece is very light and thin vs. its solid and heavy condition in raw wood. Yin and yang are hidden in the piece. 12" high, 8" diam. *Photo, artist*

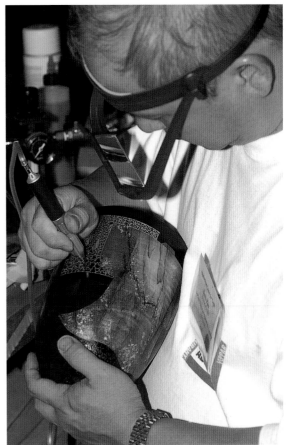

Binh Pho is shown piercing portions of a vessel using a 4,000,000 rpm Paragrave Drill because it runs fast and allows ultimate control by the artist. *Photo, artist*

William Hunter in collaboration with his wife, enamellist, Marianne Hunter. **Persian Tower**. Ebony, ivory, enamel, diamonds, and silver. This box represents a benchmark for their architectural boxes. 7" high, 4" diam. *Photo, George Post*

Davoud Khasravi. **Timelessness**. Purpleheart and maple. Several techniques are combined to create this piece that he terms, "wooden pottery." They include inlaying, laminating, turning, carving, and sanding. The many small pieces are cut and aligned in medleys of grain, color, and pattern, hand sanded, or shaped, and polished on a large lathe, then varnished to a high gloss. 34" high, 20" diam. *Courtesy, artist*

Ed Zbik. **Dragon Bowl #2**. Segmented woodturning method. Fiddleback maple background. The pattern consists of redwood lace burl, tulipwood, and mother-of-pearl. The base and rim are zircote, with a pewter inlay in the rim. *Photo, artist*

Dewey Garrett. **Red Palm**. Made from a palm wood that is usually discarded. The artist has developed methods for turning, bleaching, and dyeing the wood to accentuate its unique character. 13" high, 8" diam. *Photo, artist*

Clay Foster. **Mud Pot**. Oak. The decoration on this wood vessel is achieved by drawing the design on the wood with mud from a squeeze bottle, and then scorching the exposed wood with a torch. The mud dries and flakes off, leaving the unscorched wood design. "With the focus of many woodworkers on precision, exactness, and perfection, I chose to celebrate irregularities, casual execution, and spontaneous design. The style reflects my own life, rather than an orderly, controlled, and methodical direction." 17" high, 8" diam. *Photo, artist*

Peter M. Petrochko. **Busy Wood Series**. Sculptural vessels. Twenty different native and exotic woods. 18" high, 16" diam. Complex patterning combines laminating, band sawing, carving, and disc-sanding for exploring various relationships in form, pattern, color, and texture. *Photo, Frank Poole*

Simon Levy. **Turned Vessel**. The surface of a lathe-turned vessel is important to the artist. He uses engraving, carving, wood burning, drawing, and painting. d*el Mano Gallery, Los Angeles, California.*

Kip Christensen. **Inlaid Box**. Box elder burl, pink ivory wood. A favorite feature of this box is a gentle vacuum resistance felt when the lid is removed from the base. 3.5" high, 4.5" diam. *Photo, Photocraft*

Patti Fleming. **Bishop's Hood**. Buckeye burl and Osage orange. Based on a cactus seen in a Scottsdale, Arizona cactus garden. The realism of the colors and textures achieved in wood are quite remarkable. 7" high, 6" diam. *Photo, Bob Hawks*

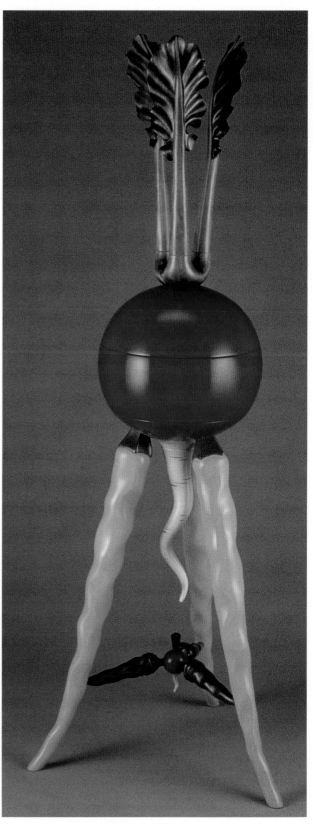

Craig Nutt. **Radish Salad Bowl**. Open. Lacquer on carved wood. Standing nearly five feet tall, this sculpture is actually a functional salad bowl. The leaves lift off to become salad servers, and the top of the radish is inverted to make a second serving bowl. 56" high, 21" wide, 17" deep. Collection, Renwick Gallery, Washington, D.C. *Photo, John Lucas*

Craig Nutt. **Radish Salad Bowl**. Closed. The leaves lift off and become the salad servers. *Photo, John Lucas*

Liam O'Neill. **Set of Three Redwood Vessels**. The front vessel is on a redwood plinth. O'Neill revels in the concept of renewal involved in bringing exciting artwork from dead trees, the only kind of wood he uses. By working on such a large scale with his outdoor pieces, his indoor work exhibits a similar monumentality on a smaller scale. Bowls 21" high, 22" diam. *Photo, Michael Blake*

Dennis Elliott. **Sculpted Vessel**. Big leaf maple burl. Turned, carved, and burned. When carving from a burl, one never knows what the interior of the log will look like and how the final item will appear. Elliott uses the so-called "imperfections" of the log to make a sculptural statement. 15" high, 19.5" diam. *Photo, Iona S. Elliott*

Working with a vessel this size is not a project to be taken lightly. The wood is heavy. Here, Dennis Elliott sands a big leaf maple burl bowl while it is on the lathe. Such vessels have become his trademark. Sometimes he incorporates other materials such as pewter, exotic woods, avonite, semi-precious stones. He bleaches or burns the wood to add drama and interest. *Photo, Iona S. Elliott*

Gary Stevens. **Vortex**. First growth redwood lace burl that is well over 1000 years old. Living in coastal California, Stevens enjoys the forest and the ocean with its constantly changing forces. He says, "In the Vortex Series, I pay tribute to the magnificence of nature's power and hope to create vessels that have a similar feel. The vortex form is always magnificent in its seemingly simple complexity." 20" high, 14" wide, 11" deep. Collection, Randy Antik. *Photo, Paul Titangos*

Gary Stevens. Steven's passion is finding rare pieces of burl wood on his property in California's Santa Cruz Mountains. Trees that were logged or burned by fire hundreds of years ago may have left stumps and burls that are thousands of years old. The barks and next layer have to be cleaned away, a laborious job done with hand tools and gloves. Then portions are cut off that will be turned into bowls. *Courtesy, artist*

A log is trucked to his studio by tractor or van, then it is hoisted into place and onto the spindle of the lathe. The rough form is shaped on the lathe. After that, the lathe is a holding device while he further carves with chain saws, grinders and other power tools. He works the wood green to its almost final stage, then lets it cure 3 to 4 months before finishing.

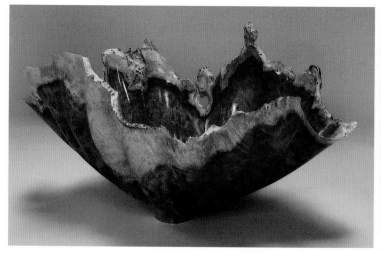

Gary Stevens. **Firedance #13**. Redwood lace burl. One of a series of turnings that appear to be erupting flames as they dance in the wind. The forms rise up from the base with earthen hues of crimson red and gold, ever curling, turning, and reaching upwards toward the sky. His entire Firedance Series explodes with energy and movement, much like a roaring campfire. *Photo, Paul Titangos*

He turns and completes a piece to about a 1/2" thickness then puts it in the drying room. When he determines it is ready, based on moisture content, weight, feel, and experience, he adds the finishing touches.

Gary Stevens' pieces are shown in a collector's living room in San Francisco, California. *Courtesy, artist.*

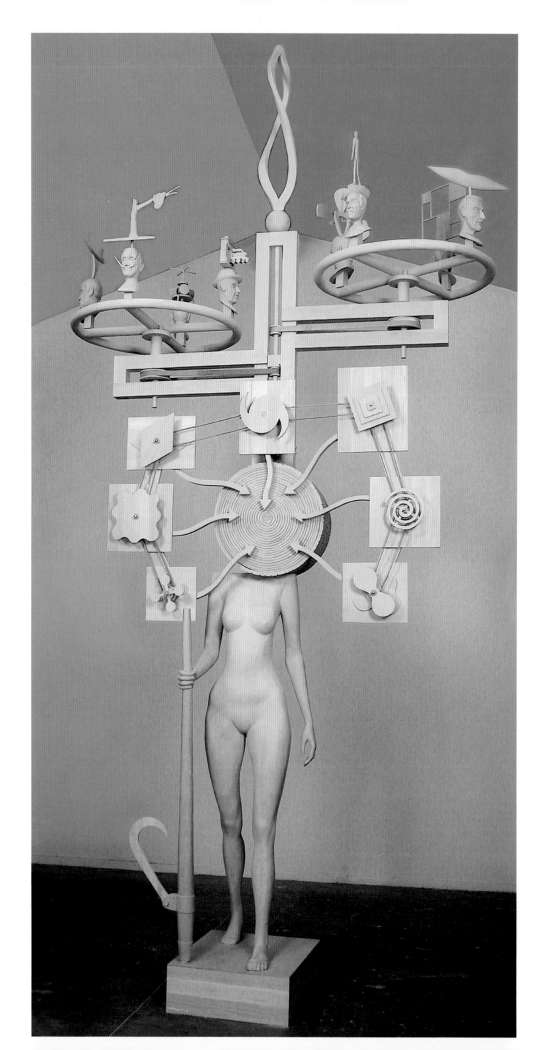

Chapter 4
Sculpture-The Wood Speaks

The carving process has become second nature to me now. I attack the wood intuitively as if almost in a trance. It is a very fast paced subtractive process, carving away material from all areas at different depths and angles. Joël Urruty

With changes in wood furniture and vessels carving out new roads in their respective territory, it's not surprising that much of that activity would spill over into sculpture. Wood turners who have spread their wings beyond the lathe's boundaries have spurred much of that activity. Coupled with that is the availability of a wide variety of power tools now used by sculptors…tools once considered only for the manual training and wood shop.

People who want to make large wood sculptures need not chisel and whittle away wood with small tools like the shoemaker Geppetto carving out his Pinocchio. The beginning of new sculptural forms with power tools was initiated in the 1930s and 40s by Henry Moore, Barbara Hepworth, Alexander Calder, Jean Arp, Constantin Brancusi, Chaim Gross, and others of that generation. They pioneered abstract wood sculptures.

Traditional forms and ideas for wood sculpture and carving have not changed significantly. There are still many variations on the human form, on animals, plants, and work inspired by primitive cultures, such as African and New Guinea pieces.

So what has changed?

Today's wood sculptors are more selectively using inspiration from these cultures. Instead of emulating the forms, they are inventing textural variations, minute carving details, wood combinations, and using more exotic woods available from other countries.

Yes, there are still sculptures based on the human form that are realistic and abstract. They still employ both carving and constructing techniques or, as the art world refers to them, subtractive (carving) and additive (constructing). There are innovations in thoughts and themes.

John Buck's greater than life-size wood sculptures often use myriad geometric shapes with the figures and carved objects, abstract and realistic. Buck works in various media, including wood, bronze, printing, and rubbings.

Elizabeth Frank's figure, *Box of Stars,* is constructed and carved from reclaimed wood and fallen aspen branches near her southern Arizona studio. Collected wood from urban scrap piles, arroyos, and remote mountains of the southwest may be teamed with antique ceiling tin, discarded jewelry, and old photographs. Inspiration may come from the materials or from popular culture, ancient stories, and forces of nature. The acts of assembling and creation often evoke forgotten memories, hu-

Opposite page:
John Buck. **Against the Grain.** Jelutong wood, leather, and a motor. Female figures involved with myriad different symbolic images recur in Buck's sculptures. This one is motorized. Jelutong is a soft white wood culled from Malaysian farming operations. It is too soft to use in the building industry but it is well suited to furniture makers and wood sculptors. Buck retains hack marks and chisel cuts to emulate a tradition of folk art, handmade crafts, and votive figures. Often, a wood sculpture is the model for a bronze sculpture. Buck also carves intricate wood blocks for printing. 180" high, 84" wide, 36" deep. *Courtesy, artist*

mor, and primordial knowledge that everyone may share. Frank, who once worked for the film industry, combines her forms with intriguing and imaginative surface decoration.

Jerry Barrish also creates figures from found objects. Some are lathe turned. They have a minimalist approach to the figure that may be anything but realistic.

Brad Sells exploits forms that he seems to "see" within a raw piece of wood to release his "people." Joël Urruty says it is natural for people to appear in his work as he's an inveterate people watcher. He captures their postures and body language, and tries to eliminate everything that is superfluous to the form he presents.

Edward Hart and Ron Koehler work from boards and use the table saw to great advantage for their figurative pieces. Michael J. Brolly, originally a self-taught turner working alone and remotely, had no influences telling him what could and could not be done. He freely mixes a turned wood element, carving, mechanical joints, and old wood working techniques to create a peculiar and often humorous sculpture that, incidentally, may be functional. He was among the early artists who helped blur the line between container and sculpture and didn't even realize it.

Giles Gilson begins with a concept and develops pure sculpture. Where Brolly contrasts woods for color and impact, Gilson finishes his abstract female figures, dressed in formal clothes, in high gloss paints and acrylics.

Architectural forms, and wood pierced with other materials, are in pieces by Robyn Horn and Richard Hooper. Michelle Holzapfel brilliantly tackles the challenge of carving shapes and concepts that would defy most carvers. She carves intricate knots, tassels, and other fiber oriented images. Many pieces in her prodigious output are based on literary images. Arthur Jones studies the undersea marine life for his forms and develops them in variations of lathe made shapes to which he adds delicate carving.

The human form, flora, fauna, and abstractions are only a few of the topics that come under the tools of the talented wood worker. Their amazing art objects are based on geometric shapes, on the use of negative vs. positive shapes, on ideas suggested by the wood, on imagination, and on successful innovative applications of the tools themselves. Curved forms may evolve from experimentation with a new tool. Often the acquisition of a new tool or an accessory, and new capabilities will lead an artist into an entirely fresh direction. In some instances, the desire to do something different will inspire the artist to develop a new tool. Other techniques shown are piercing, deconstruction and reassembling, and working with small sculptural forms for making netsuke.

Wood sculptures are mostly designed for indoor use because of the tendency for wood to deteriorate over time. Look for large works in public spaces such as malls and office building lobbies, in museums and galleries. Smaller works may be found in these same venues and in many private collections.

John Buck. **Honomolino Series.** Koa wood. The human figure appears in many of Buck's sculptures and they are always involved with balancing objects in surrealistic relationships. 93.5" high, 123" wide, 39" deep. *Courtesy, artist*

Joël Urruty. **We**. Mahogany, bleached oak, and milk paint. A geometric shape is combined with abstract figures to create a relationship that evokes clarity and mystery. The figures are hand carved with incised lines. 18.25" high, 23" wide, 7.25" deep. *Photo, Pat Simione*

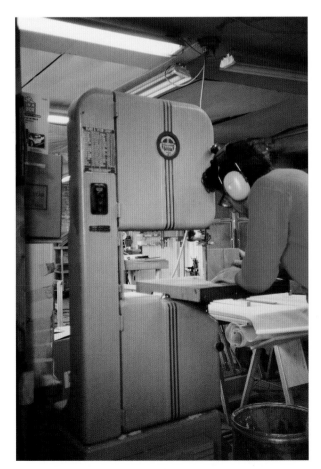

Joël Urruty's studio has an assortment of hand and power tools required to create an unending variety of art. Urruty makes sculptures, vessels, and furniture. Here, he uses a band saw to cut out a blank for the sculpture, "We." *Photo, Pat Simione*

He roughs out the sculptural shape using a carbide tough blade on an electric grinder. Lines and shapes are smoothed out using fine grit sanding discs on an electric sander. *Photo, Pat Simione*

David Groth. **Guardian #2.** Myrtlewood burl carved with a chainsaw. Groth uses massive logs he reclaims from beaches near his studio in northern California. His chainsaw carving process is intuitive and requires complete concentration. Once the wood is removed, it can't be put back; each sculpture is carved from a single block. About 45" high, 23" wide, 15" deep. *Photo, artist*

David Groth's Abstract Chain Saw Sculptures

We have seen how artists who make vessels take their chain saws into the forests to unearth stumps and find burls from which they can make their forms. The sculptor, too, is always on the lookout for large pieces of dead wood in which a sculpture might be encased much like an archeologist digging to find meaningful artifacts of an early culture.

In the following series, David Groth takes the reader on a journey from collecting the wood, through the procedures required to chain saw carve and finish an abstract sculpture. This differs from the techniques used by those who make vessels. The vessel maker depends on a lathe and may use other tools. The sculptor uses a variety of tools and the use of a lathe may be incidental or may not be used at all.

1. David Groth illustrates his procedure and the steps involved in creating his large sculptures. He begins by collecting the wood burl at the beach for a sculpture that will be titled Dragon #2 (shown at the end of the series) and trucked to his studio.
Photo series, courtesy artist

2. Groth prepares the log by trimming away the outer bark and inner soft layers with hand tools before he can begin carving with the chain saw.

3. When he feels and sees the form within he begins to carve with the chain saw.

189

4. He must focus completely on evolving the form, a process that requires total concentration.

5. The shape emerges.

6. Negative areas are created.

7. In addition to a chain saw, a variety of power tools, such as sanders and grinders may be used for finishing.

8. Final texturing and finishing are done with hand tools. Below is the finished sculpture.

David Groth. **Dragon #2**. Myrtlewood burl carved with a chain saw. Groth explains that a body of work, such as the pieces illustrated, are part of a continuum, with each sculpture always leading to the next. *Photo, artist*

191

The Human Form

Since the beginning of time, man has created sculpture in his own image. Early Greek and Roman sculptures prove this point. The human as subject matter can be more creative than the subject itself. Some techniques and materials used in the pieces that follow are by direct carving, and by construction. They may employ a variety of found objects as well as fresh lumber and logs, and scrap logs and branches.

Elizabeth Frank. **Box of Stars**. (Detail.) Carved wood and mixed media. Reclaimed wood and found objects. 73" high, 16" wide 16" deep. *Photo, Jeff Smith*

Joël Urruty **Compassion II**. Mahogany, oak, steel, and milk paint. Color used in this piece represents unity and division. The patterns differ representing individuality, yet they are complimentary intensifying one another. 68" high, 22" wide, 18" deep. *Photo, Pat Simione*

Joël Urruty. **Totem: A Torso.** Mahogany, oak, and milk paint. The lines in the figures create a puzzle-like pattern suggesting scarification. The lines represent scars from life, and individual accumulated experiences. The chaotic geometric pattern creates a visual contrast with the organic form on which it is incised. 26" high, 6" wide, 8" deep. *Photo, Pat Simione*

Brad Sells. **Figure Group**. Apple, Osage orange, and dogwood. 45 to 55" high. *Photo, John Lucas*

Jerry Ross Barrish. **American Painter**. Assemblage of found wood and plastic. The pieces are straight and spindle turned, with carved and fabricated parts. 49" high, 13" wide, 13" deep. *Photo, Mel Schockner*

Edward Hart. **Dancers Three**. Oak, walnut, rosewood, and Malaysian apitong. The challenge is to make wood appear to move gracefully, using simple forms. 5' tall, 34" wide, 12" deep. *Photo, artist*

Ron Koehler. **Family.** Assembled wood with movable elements forms an amazing installation. The sculpture is life size. *Photo, artist*

Michael J. Brolly. **www.jewel@space.re**. Mahogany, maple, purpleheart, ebony, bubinga, sterling silver, gold, gold leaf, feathers, bicycle parts, bearings, brass, and Delron. Her leg joints have bicycle quick releases so that one can change her height. Her face slides back on a Delron track. Her pierced tongue can hold ten pairs of earrings. The bra cups revolve out and hold earrings. The drawers revolve on bearings and have magnets to keep them lined up in the closed position. Her teeth and tongue slide out. 55-59" high, 10" wide, 16" deep. *Photo, David Hass*

Michael J. Brolly. (Detail of mouth open.) Although this is also a container for jewelry, it satisfies the sculpture concept because of its form and artistic conception. Collection, Fleur Bressler. *Photo, David Hass*

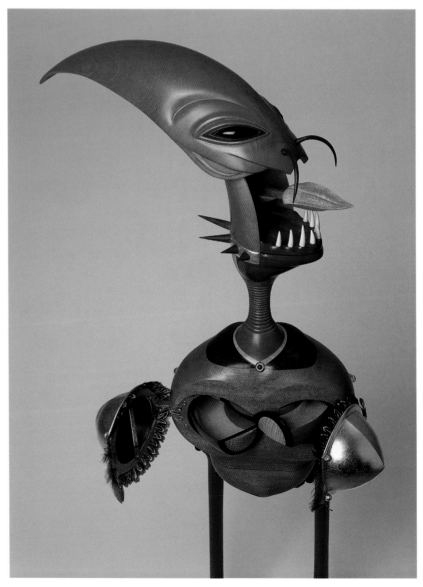

Michael J. Brolly. **A Couple of Birthday Suits**. Mahogany and PVC pipe. Made for a group show entitled "The Birthday Party." 25" high, 12" wide, 12" deep. *Photo, David Hass*

Giles Gilson. **The Child Within.** Closed. Feather Sculpture, pedestal piece. Mahogany case, lacquered basswood, white pearl with orange/magenta toning, figured maple, East Indian rosewood, ebony, holly, padouk, stainless steel, and black acrylic. 26" high, 18" wide, 12" deep. *Photo, artist*

Giles Gilson. **The Child Within**. Open.

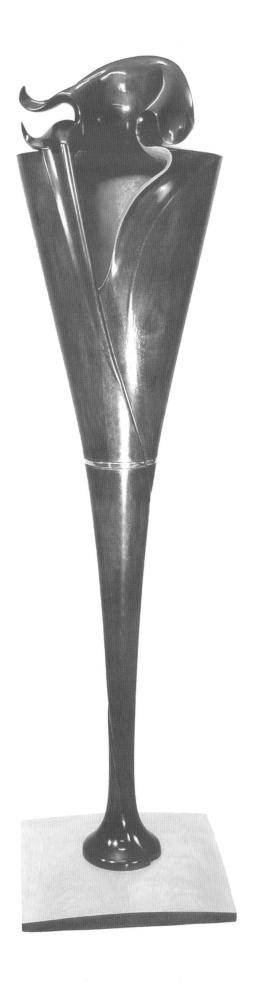

Giles Gilson. **Cammy-Oh 9. Highlights from the Muse.** Enriched walnut, blue interior, brass ring, and figured birch foot. This is the 9th in a series of sculpture inspired by a friend. It is the same height as the young woman and the spiral line from lapel to foot is modeled after her. The idea is to imply types of people by suggesting clothing on turned objects. It is a vertical form with a sharp shoulder, a sassy left lapel, and a bold collar. 63.5" high, 16" diam. *Photo, artist*

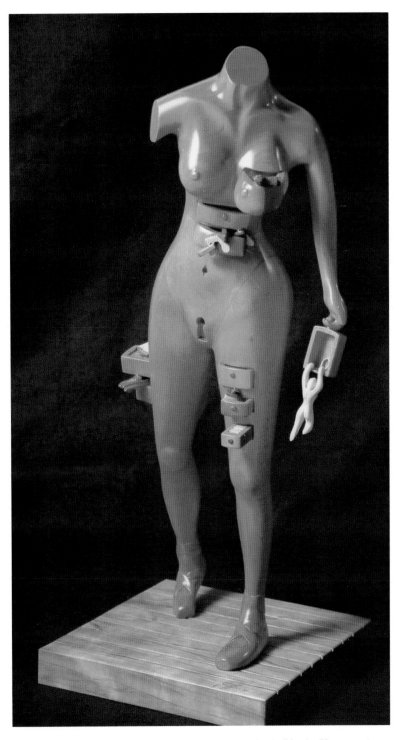

Philippe Guillerm. **Memories.** Mahogany and maple. 31" high. *Photo, artist*

199

Architectural Forms

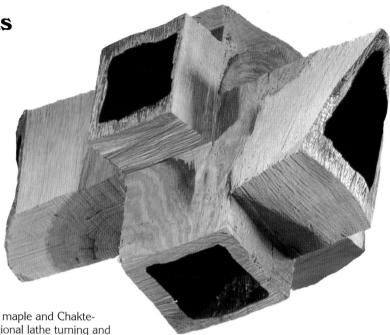

Jack R. Slentz. **Cantilevered**. Oak. These pieces are architecturally based. 11" high, 17" wide, 11" deep. *Photo, Sean Moorman*

Tex Isham. **The Wedge**. Side view. Bleached maple and Chakte-kok. Isham is intrigued by starting with traditional lathe turning and off-center turning, and then abstracting and cutting apart shapes to create geometric abstract forms. These shapes rely on light and shadows, giving a static structure a dynamic intensity. 10.5" high, 9" wide, 3" deep. *Photo, David Peters*

Tex Isham. **The Wedge**. Front view. *Photo, David Peters*

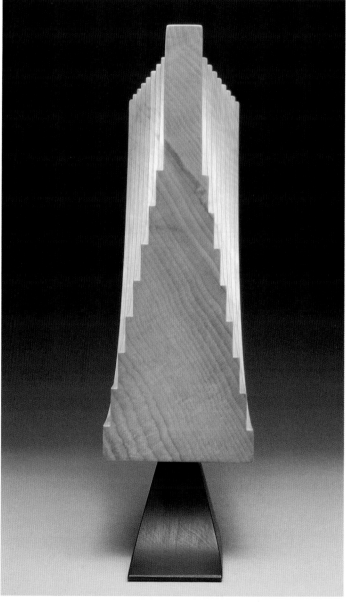

Peter M. Petrochko. **Split Wood/Band Saw Series**. Black walnut. An architectural feeling with all smooth planes disassembled and reassembled. 9" high, 4" wide, 5" deep. Collection John and Robyn Horn. *Photo, Frank Poole*

Peter M. Petrochko. **Split Wood/Band Saw Series**. White ash. Combines and opposes textures using bark and smooth areas. 18" high 3" diam. at bottom, 4" diam. at top. *Photo, Frank Poole*

Jack R. Slentz. **Mayan**. Red oak. 39" high, 23" wide, 20" deep. *Photo, Sean Moorman*

201

Jack R. Slentz. **Installation**. **Pura Vida.** Pieces are made of cherry, sweet gum, and ash. The simple forms in these pieces reflect the core similarities we all have; to be loved, needed, respected, and understood. But the exteriors have different textures much like our individual personalities. 9.5" high, 17' wide, 15' deep. *Photo, artist*

Dewey Garrett. **Parallax in Red and Black**. Ebonized oak with acrylic paint. This piece involved a complicated process of assembly, turning, and reassembly. The segmented design presents ever-changing views and moiré-like patterns as the observer changes positions. 11" high, 8" wide, 4" deep. *Photo, artist*

Peter M. Petrochko. **The Opening**. Split Wood Series. Madrone with an African wenge base. 21" high, 14" wide, 8" deep. Collection, John and Robyn Horn. *Photo, Frank Poole*

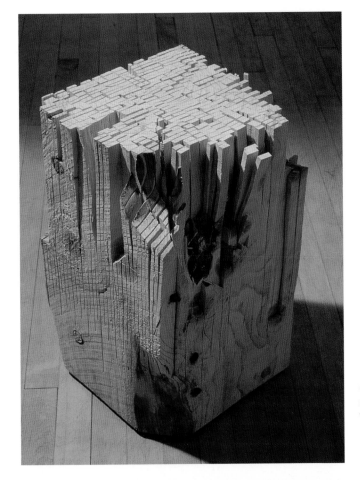

Christopher McNulty. **Measure V.** From a series of sculptures created by repeatedly dividing a space or volume into a non-standard series of units. 19" high, 12" wide, 12" deep. *Photo, William Lemke*

Dennis Elliott. **Gemini Vortex**. Big leaf maple burl with stainless steel. One in an "orbital" series in which the viewer can turn the sculpture on its base to see it from all sides. 29.5" high, 20.5" wide, 5" deep. *Photo, Iona S. Elliott*

Glenn Elvig. **Legends VI.** Maple burl with mahogany. This piece was a backlash at the popular use of the lathe for just making bowl forms. 10.5" high, 8" wide, 7" deep. *Courtesy, artist*

Richard Hooper. **Q Form**. Birch plywood. Hooper explains, "This sculpture reflects my interest in balance, perhaps a formal minimal expression of my childhood interest in gymnastics, a Euclidean headstand maybe?" 14" long, 2" deep. *Photo, Bob Baxter*

Robyn Horn. **Arched Pierced Stone.** Coolibah burl and steel. Horn's sculpture, beginning with a turned wood form, was then pierced with a sheet of steel conveying a contrast of geometric line and of material. 5" high, 9" wide, 6" deep. *Photo, Sean Moorman*

Curves and Twists

Jean-Christophe Couradin. **D'Amourette**. Cocobolo. Sinuous curves and smooth textures in a wood with beautiful grain result in a sculpture that is tactile and sensual. 20" long. *Photo, Daniel Guillous*

Richard Hooper. **Embryo**. Birch plywood with acrylic paint. Although entitled Embryo, in fact this form originated as a distillation of a 'Klein bottle' (a mathematical model of a three dimensional form) with only one surface. This carved piece was reshaped several times before the final shape was achieved. 9" high, 15" wide, 7" deep. *Photo, Bob Baxter*

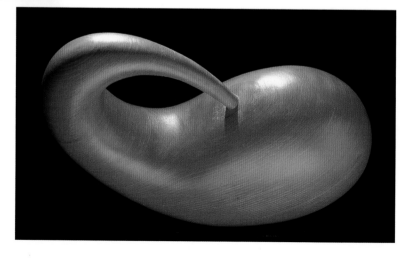

Richard Hooper. **Infinity**. Birch plywood. This is the first piece he did that exploited computer aided design and manufacture. It is a complex three-dimensional form based on the Infinity symbol. It was laminated on a thirty-degree angle to modulate the plywood orientation and vary the visual character of the laminate. 5" high, 14" wide, 7" deep. *Photo, Bob Baxter*

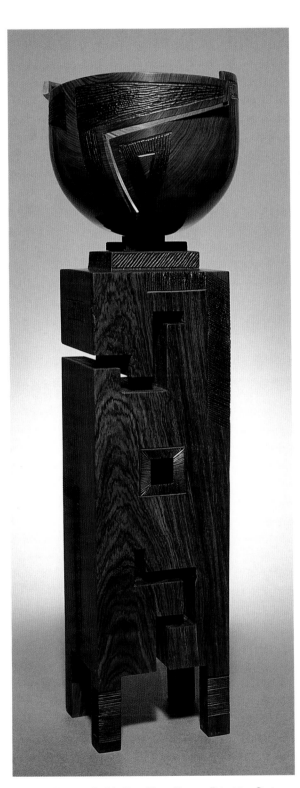

William Hunter. **Spirit Dwelling**. Future Primitive Series. Cocobolo, ink, and gold leaf. The cut vessel was designed to spring apart and to add a tension to the sculpture. 26" high, 8" wide. *Photo, George Post*

William Hunter. **Cutting Loose**. Cocobolo. This piece refers to the abstract skew chisel (the base) cutting into the sacred circle and having it seem to fly apart. It reflected his personal feelings about his work at the time and also about the turning field in general. 23.5" high, 10.5 in. wide, 10.5" deep. Collection of the Mint Museum, Charlottesville, North Carolina. *Photo, Hap Sakwa*

William Hunter. **Tangled Helix**. Cocobolo. The two part sculpture is an interactive piece that the viewer is urged to re-arrange and reconfigure to energize space. 10" high, 32" long, 15" deep. *Photo, Hap Sakwa*

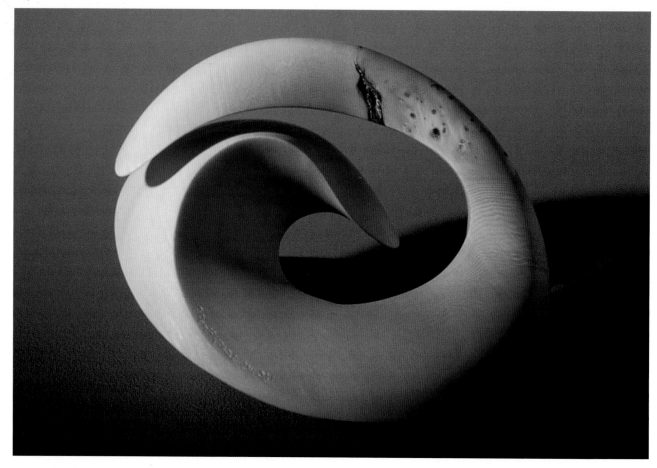

Rémi Verchot. **Wave**. Tasmanian Huon pine. The artist bypasses heavily grained wood or burls in favor of materials that do not interrupt the form itself. He may sandblast a piece or show the grain when the grain and the form enhance one another. 4" diam. *Photo, Angelea Moser*

Arthur Jones. **Counterpoint.** Camphor. Carved. Based on the unfolding forms in a lily bloom. 13" long, 5" diam. Collection, Roger Ford. *del Mano Gallery. Los Angeles, California. Photo, artist*

Arthur Jones. **Schism**. Mahogany. Turned and carved with the carved elements posed in opposite directions. While they suggest conflict, the elements join to form an oblique circle, a symbol of unity. 8" high, 16" long. Collection, Caroline Stevens. *Photo, artist*

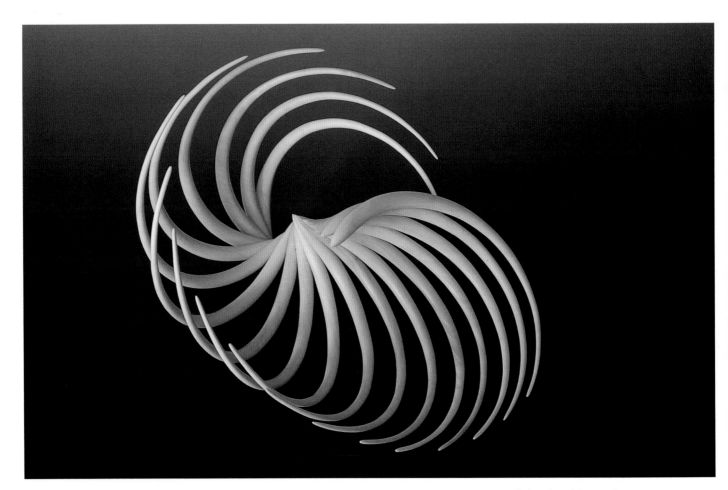

Arthur Jones. **Ribbed Molluscus**. Tulipwood. Based on the idea that a mutant specie of clam has left its calcareous shell to enjoy life as a vertebrate. He conjures how something might appear if it were other that what it is normally known to be. The piece is light in appearance, fragile, and delicate exhibiting order, symmetry, repetition, and movement. 7" high, 12" wide, 9.5" deep. Collection, Larry and Myrna Seale. *Photo, artist*

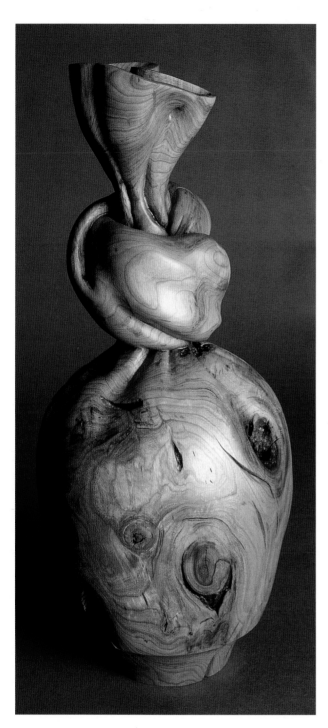

Michelle Holzapfel. **Peter's Knot Vase**. Maple burl. Making a knot was a reaction to the trend of turning thin-walled vessels. She continues to create knots because they are visually and esthetically intriguing, and have multiple associations. 19" high, 13" wide, 11" deep. Barry Friedman Ltd. Gallery. *Photo, David Holzapfel*

Michelle Holzapfel. **Tasseled Vase**. Butternut burl. The vase, knot, and rope, are carved from one piece of wood. 12" high, 10" wide, 6" deep. *Photo, David Holzapfel*

Michelle Holzapfel

Michelle Holzapfel has carved out a career in astonishing directions. Most obvious are the examples that follow, along with the techniques and talents required to produce a body of gutsy, strong pieces. She was raised learning to make turnings on her father's metal lathe that she still uses. Her familiarity and dexterity with the unit has enabled her to use the lathe freely, and freehand, to create compound curves and elegant forms in her bowls and sculptures. Her pieces often are based on ideas, forms, spacing, and compositions from classical architectural ornament, and literary and musical references.

In her early work, Holzapfel often championed the role of women in the male dominated wood turning milieu and brought it to fruition. Following her example, today there are many women wood turners who excel at their art.

Michelle Holzapfel. **Peter's Knot**. Holzapfel wanted a sculpture that would be only the knot. Not an easy concept to evolve from a solid burl. Here's one view of the piece towards which she was working.

The sculpture began as a large burl on which she wrote "big knot" as a reminder.

Holzapfel roughs out the form and plans the way a knot occupies space. It has no fixed top or bottom and must be carved on every surface.

She lays out the spiral rope lines so they look convincing.

Carving the rope shapes and deepening the v-cuts.

The strands are smoothed and the ends are opened. The binding at the other end is carved.

Michelle Holzapfel. **Peter's Knot**. The final knot; another view. The piece was named for a nautical friend who was living his last days as she worked on the piece. *Photo series, David Holzapfel*

Terry Martin. **Emerging Cyclops**. Redgum. The piece deals with the idea that what we make is buried in the wood waiting to be uncovered. This solid piece is acknowledgment of the trees from which both material and inspiration are obtained. The technical challenge of turning a 200-lb. piece of wood with an uneven balance is complicated. At the rim the piece is turned for only part of its diameter. Even the central section is fully turned, not carved. 21" high, 19" wide, 9" deep. *Photo, Russell Stokes*

Terry Martin. **Carved Cyclops.** Jarrah. The central pierced, turned element, the Cyclops, is a vessel for light and air. It is the antitheses of the functional vessel and is the focus for a series of different designs that explore the lift and elevation of the central eye. 13" high. *Photo, Russell Stokes*

Ben Trupperbäumer. **Muricidae**. A shell form hand carved. *del Mano Gallery, Los Angeles, California. Photo, David Peters*

Ben Trupperbäumer. **Muricidae**. A sea creature interpreted in mahogany. *del Mano Gallery, Los Angeles, California. Photo, David Peters*

Alain Mailland. Mailland works with the secret wonders of burls and roots of the south of France. He specializes in greenwood hollowing, then further carves the forms to result in hybrid vegetation, animal, or cosmic creatures, and suggests that you see what you like in them. *Photo, artist*

Alain Mailland. **Babel II**. Arbute tree root. 10.25" high, 5" diam.

Alain Mailland. **Eclosion**. Elm. 14" high, 14" diam. Bohlen Collection. *Photo, artist*

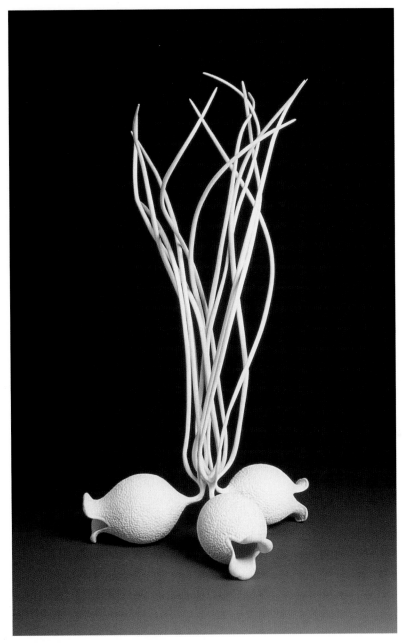

Alain Mailland. **The Soul Sisters**. Hackberry. 4" high. Collection, Musée des Pays de l´Ain, France. *Photo, Daniel Guilloux*

Alain Mailland. **So Many Mouths to Feed**. Juniper burl. 20" high, 10" diam. *Photo, artist*

Steve Loar with Johannes Michelsen. **New This Season**:
Michelsenius Loararia Robustus. Madrone burl, walnut box elder,
horn, bamboo, and brass. Created as the table centerpiece for *The
Birthday Party,* an international invitation theme exhibition at the
Brand Library and Arts Center, Glendale, California, in March 2001.
60" high, 22" diam. *Photo, David Moheny*

Steve Loar with Mark Sfirri, David Ellsworth, John Jordan, and Kim
Conover-Loar. **...and They Came Bearing Gifts**. Mahogany, ash,
box elder, redwood burl, purpleheart, and mixed media. The piece
by Steve Loar is composed of components originally shaped by the
contributing artists and then altered. 53" high, 38" wide, 24" deep.
Photo, Dubois/Tower.

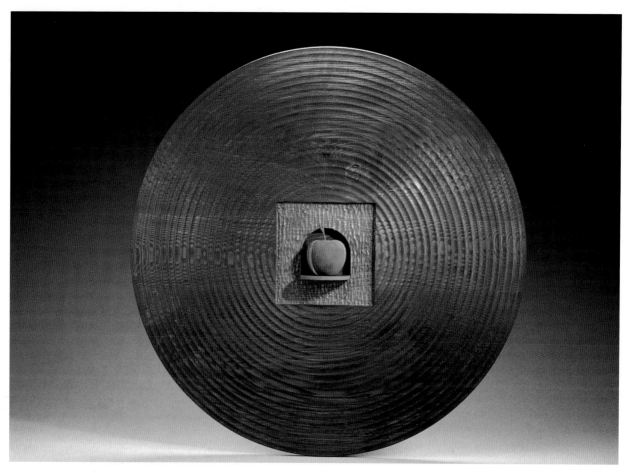

Merryll Saylan. **Forbidden Fruit.** Ash and maple. Saylan has always been interested in employing "still life" themes in her work. In this piece, the "forbidden" apple has been bronzed with paint. 2" high, 27" diam. *Photo, Hap Sakwa*

Merryll Saylan. **Moon Over Marsh**. Mahogany and milk paint. 1.5" high, 28" diam. *Photo, Hap Sakwa*

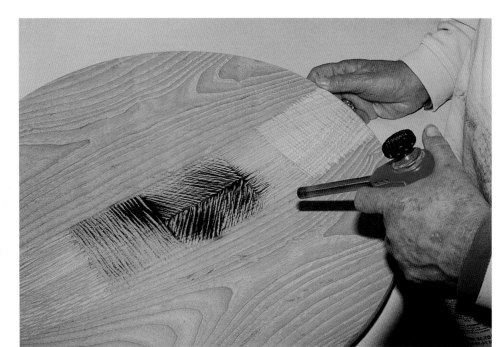

Merryll Saylan achieves unique textures and colors using a variety of techniques; most unusual are her methods for dying, charring, and carving a surface. She chars the wood with a propane torch.

Dyes are added.

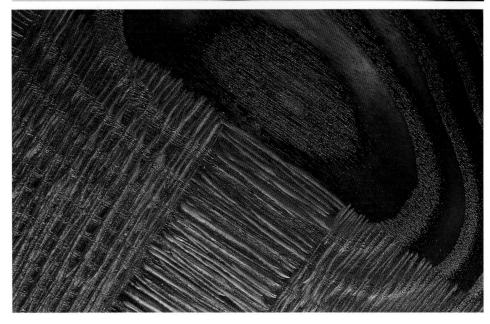

The surface is carved so that a dark and light striated effect results. Because she lives next to a tidal marsh, her surfaces are abstract interpretations of landscape and patterns.

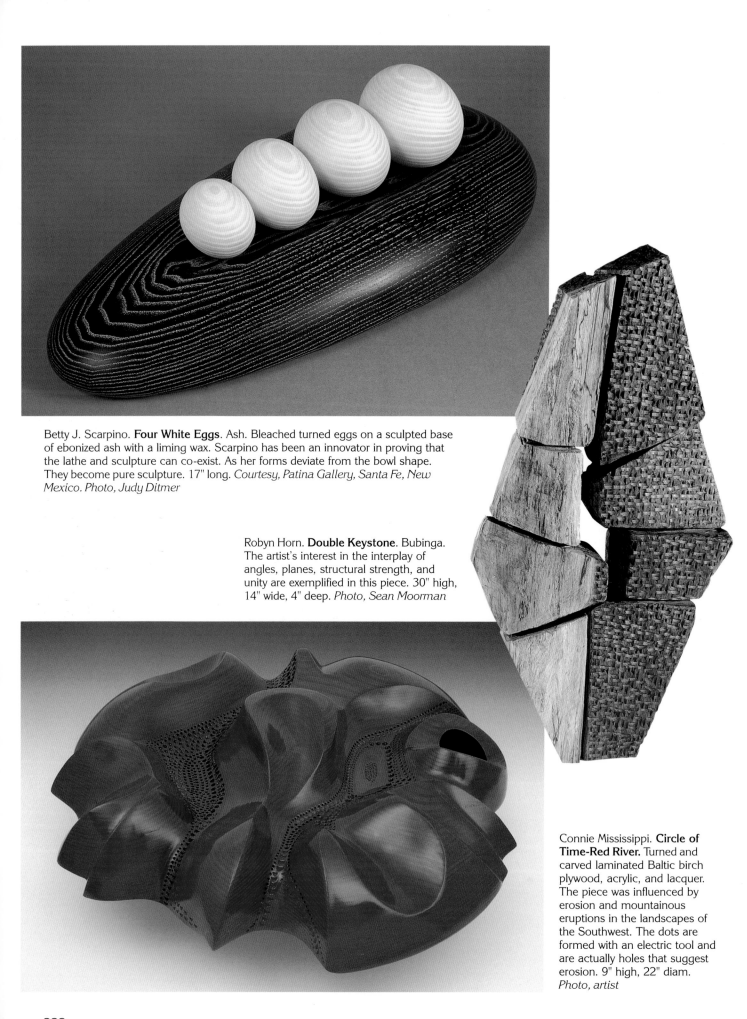

Betty J. Scarpino. **Four White Eggs**. Ash. Bleached turned eggs on a sculpted base of ebonized ash with a liming wax. Scarpino has been an innovator in proving that the lathe and sculpture can co-exist. As her forms deviate from the bowl shape. They become pure sculpture. 17" long. *Courtesy, Patina Gallery, Santa Fe, New Mexico. Photo, Judy Ditmer*

Robyn Horn. **Double Keystone**. Bubinga. The artist's interest in the interplay of angles, planes, structural strength, and unity are exemplified in this piece. 30" high, 14" wide, 4" deep. *Photo, Sean Moorman*

Connie Mississippi. **Circle of Time-Red River.** Turned and carved laminated Baltic birch plywood, acrylic, and lacquer. The piece was influenced by erosion and mountainous eruptions in the landscapes of the Southwest. The dots are formed with an electric tool and are actually holes that suggest erosion. 9" high, 22" diam. *Photo, artist*

222

Michael R. Foster. **Untitled**. Curly maple and bronze. Foster taps into the influence of early Asian, African, and Meso-American cultures to create works in wood and bronze casting. He strives to recapture the universal spirituality of those earlier works while reflecting conflicts in our modern lives. Combining these diverse mediums causes the surface to mirror opposites such as: modern vs. primitive, textured vs. smooth, industrial vs. natural, or tranquility vs. agitation. 17" high, 12" diam. *Photo, artist*

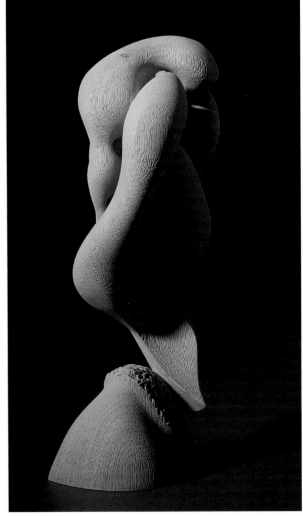

Rémi Verchot. **De l'un à l'autre**. An expression that means, loosely, "tell it to someone else." Australian white beech, sandblasted. 12.5" high, 4.75" wide. del Mano Gallery. *Photo, Angelo Moser*

David Sengal. **Fish Monger.** Ebonized fir, sassafras, walnut, rose thorn, trifoliate orange thorns, and crab claws for the bird's beak. Turned, carved, and sandblasted. The bird is turned hollow and has a small lid on its back. There are 57 fish on the vessel that is more sculpture than vessel. 20" high, 8" diam. *Courtesy, artist*

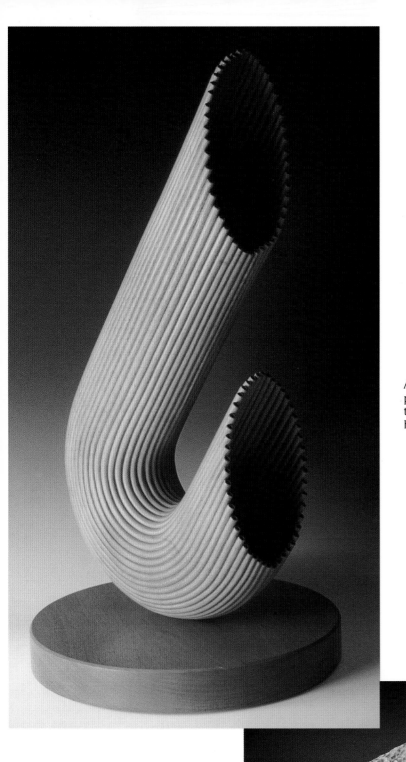

Arthur Jones. **Tube Coral**. Carved mahogany. Nature's coral provides the inspiration for this sculpture that combines textured ridges, but the ridges themselves are smooth. 27" high, 5.75" side, 13" deep. *Photo, artist*

Terry Martin. **Bonsai**. Coolibah. This is a fully sculptured piece. No lathe work was used. The "leaves" consist of the natural stippled surface of the burl's exterior. The color of the "leaves" is natural but it differs from the rest of the burl because it is the sapwood. The idea of making "trees" to make trees, is a kind of irony he enjoys. Collection, Robert Bohlen. 7.5" high. *Photo, Russell Stokes.*

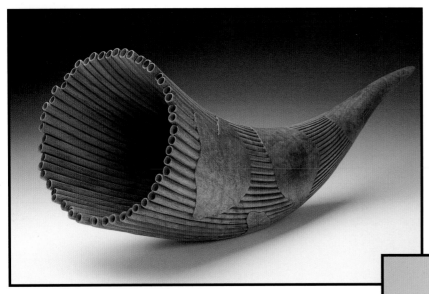

Arthur Jones. **Pipe Coral Colony**. Camphor. Inspired by a sea shell with algae formations on its surface. 6" high, 16.5" wide, 5" deep. *Photo, artist*

Michelle Holzapfel. **Reunion Bowl.** Ebonized walnut. A bowl and linked spoons, all cut from one burl, are based on a traditional tribal African spoon figure. Here the spoons are hanging down, but they could be straight out, or their positions rearranged. 28" high, 20" wide, 8" deep. *Photo, David Holzapfel*

Peter M. Petrochko. **Butterfly.** Goncalo alves with an African wenge center. The piece began as a round form, was then cut in quarters, and the ends of one of the quarters were cut off to create the form. 15" high, 11.5" wide, 30" long. Collection John and Robyn Horn. *Photo, Frank Poole*

Robert Levin. **Bundle**. Glass, wood, rope, bamboo, copper, and string. Wood combined with other media results in a unique sculpture. The different materials interact to create references that are both primitive and contemporary. 13" high, 38" wide, 14" deep. *Photo, artist*

Robert Levin. **Passage.** Glass, wood, rope, and copper. Using wood as the major component, the artist achieves a balance of form and materials. The various textures act to set off the natural qualities of the wood as an organic material. 25" high, 53" wide, 10" deep. *Photo, artist*

Michelle Holzapfel. **Death and the Maiden.** Vase. Cherry burl. The piece is based on a poem by Matthias Claudius that Schubert later put to music. In Schubert, there is an imaginary dialogue between death and the maiden, and Holzapfel captures their images in her carving. She also used pyrography to achieve the finished textures and tones. 14" high, 14" wide. 6" deep. *Photo, David Holzapfel*

Michelle Holzapfel begins by roughing out the burl to the approximate shape of the finished piece. *Photo series, David Holzapfel*

The maiden emerges from the burl under the skilled carving of the artist.

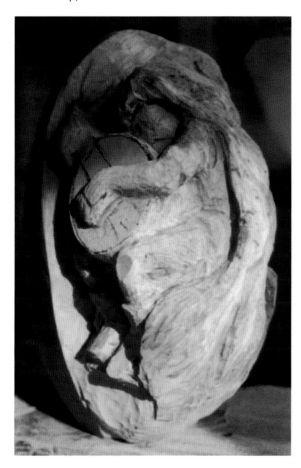

Death, personified as a lute player, is on the other side of the burl.

The figure is almost finished, but the entire piece must be further refined, and coated with Danish oil and Minwax Antique Oil finish.

Michelle Holzapfel. **Pandora's Box**. Basswood. Five panels were carved on the outside to represent an upholstered, sewn-together vessel with lid. Five different figures were carved on the inside of the panels. 15" high, 11" diam. *Photo, David Holzapfel*

Below:
Michelle Holzapfel. **Pandora's Box.** A view of the interior before the panels were sewn up. There's an upside-down serpent figure, a cat-woman, a hanging bat figure, and a tree/man, and mermaid, not shown. *Photo, David Holzapfel*

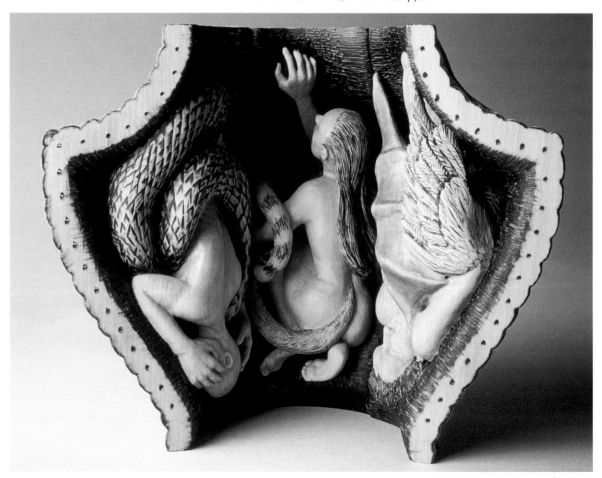

David Carlin. **The Circus.** Carved and colored netsuke 3.5" high. *del Mano Gallery, Los Angeles, California. Photo, artist*

David Carlin. **Madame Butterfly.** Carved and colored netsuke. 2.5" high. *del Mano Gallery, Los Angeles, California. Photo, artist*

David Carlin. **The Acrobat's Drama.** Carved and colored netsuke. 3.75" high. *del Mano Gallery, Los Angeles, California. Photo, artist*

Janel Jacobson **Pear Peepers**. The pear is made of pear wood. The frogs are boxwood with inlays of amber, and gold. Jacobson's inspiration comes from the natural world around her rural home. 2.8" high, 1.25" wide, 1.35" deep. *Photo, artist*

Glenn Elvig. **Fan Burl**. Spalted myrtle wood burl made into a fan form for a dramatic wall hanging. 36" high, different widths. *Courtesy, artist*

Below:
Dennis Elliott. **Wall Sculpture**. Big leaf maple burl. Turned, carved, burned. These forms are turned from protruding maple burl caps that can be cut off without harming the tree. The circle refers to the annual rings of the tree; it also symbolizes time, wholeness, and the tradition of the tondo in Western religious art. 37" high, 47" wide 2" deep. *Photo, Iona S. Elliott*

Wall Sculptures

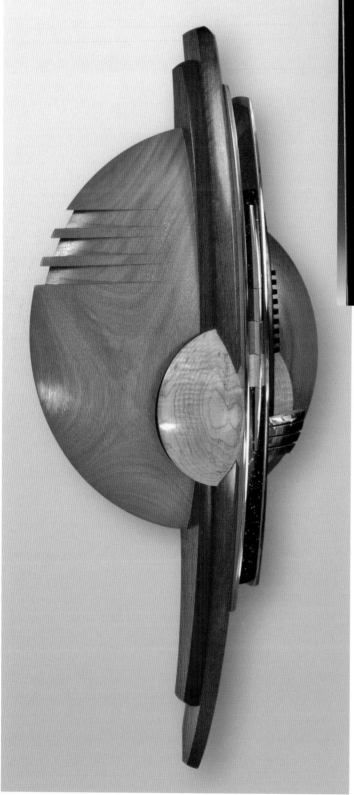

Robyn Horn. **Panel Discussion.** Wall sculpture. Cherry wood panels, carved, and burned, with a rusted finish steel frame. This piece is a commentary on the exchange of ideas and views when panelists convey their expertise on art. 34" high, 32" wide. *Photo, Sean Moorman*

Left:
Roger Heitzman. **Perihelion.** Wall sculpture. Wood, aluminum and Corian. Heitzman combines his fondness for curves and flowing forms with combinations of intersecting planes and spheres. 45" high, 19" wide. *Courtesy, artist*

Opposite page:
Nicola Henshaw. **Relief panel.** Green oak. One of three panels commissioned for the exterior wall of Low Parks Museum, Hamilton, England. The panels illustrate the history of Hamilton from its early market town days (shown here) through its industrial mining period. Etched copper plates on each panel tell the town's history. The copper plates were designed and made by sixth year students during community workshops hosted by the artist at the Glasgow print studios. Each panel is 59" high, 40" wide, 4" deep. *Photo, Andréa Nelki*

Liam O'Neill. **Ancient Cauldron**. Oak. Turned wood on a plinth.
Cauldron is 31" high, 32" diam. The plinth is 14" high. *del Mano Gallery,*
Los Angeles, California.. Photo, Michael Blake

John Boomer. **Sounding**. Walnut, oak, pine, African
wenge, sand, acrylic, and steel string. This is a sound
sculpture. 37.5" high, 15" wide, 12" deep. *Photo, artist*

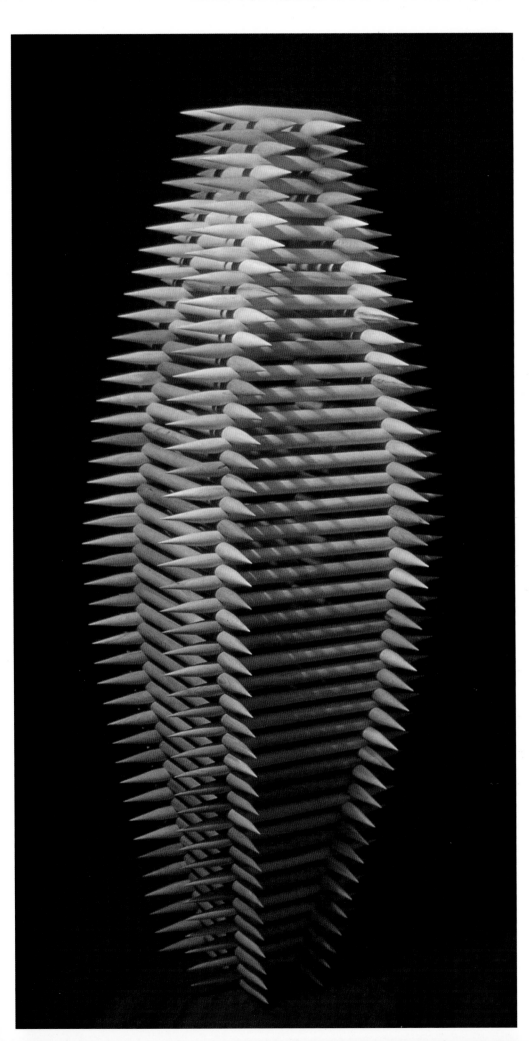

Eric Sauvé. **Untitled**. Maple. This piece is among several sculptures he has done exploring tensions between fear and curiosity and of seduction and repulsion. It represents attractiveness and aggression. He began with a full scale drawing, over 5 feet. All pieces were cut to length, and shaped to points using a jig he built for the purpose. Each piece is grooved to house and lock in place the previous row. 64" high, 24" diam. *Photo, artist*

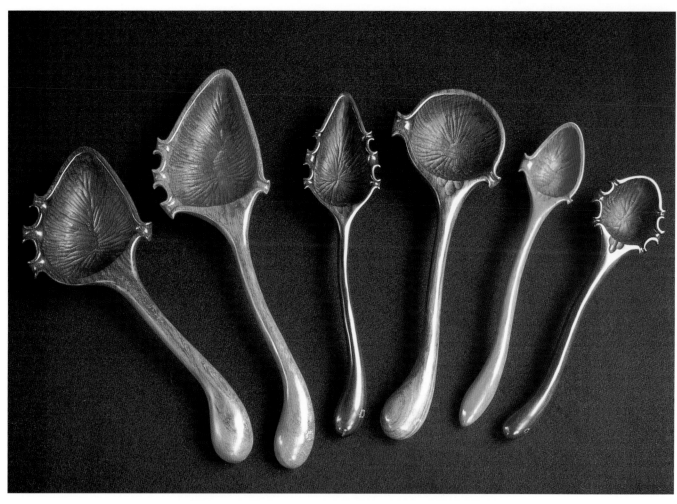

William V. Chappelow. **Multi-spouted Spoon Group**. Hand Carved spoons as functional sculpture. Left to right: Brazilian rosewood, purpleheart, East Indian rosewood, pink ivory, and ebony. *Tryyn Gallery, Guatay, California. Photo, artist*

Chapter 5
Sculptural Objects

I am continually drawn back to the smaller scale of the box. Perhaps it's the intimacy of the small, the freedom to experiment without a huge risk in time and materials, or the selfishness of relative immediate gratification.
William McDowell

The one-of-a-kind sculpted wood object with a specific purpose has become a source for artistic exploration and expression. Just as furniture is functional sculpture, so it is with small objects such as spoons, boxes, hair ornaments, jewelry, reliquaries, table pieces, toys, signage; the list is as infinite as the clever ideas in the minds of as many wood artists.

The objects that follow are only a sampling of what is available, and of the many photos submitted for the book. Many artists make a few such objects along with furniture and other items. Some concentrate on only the one form.

Both William V. Chappelow and Norm Sartorius have specialized in making sculptural wood spoons for many years and the pieces illustrate their expertise. Chappelow has his studio/shop in a small southern California town where people wend their way up the curvy road to find it. It could pass for a Santa's workshop. Within are spoons, scoops, and myriad utensils from plain, sensuously curved shapes to intricately formed and decorated pieces. He is surrounded by colorful selections of the woods he uses (see page 15).

Norm Sartorius says that for the past twelve years he has explored the potential of spoons as a context for sculpture; non-functional decorative art items that are widely collected by woodcraft enthusiasts and smart museum curators. His spoons are sensual to look at and touch. They are graceful and balanced. You can sense the artist's emotions about a piece when you handle it.

Are they sculpture or containers? Where, how do they open? These are questions Giles Gilson deals with when people see his jewelry containers in gallery displays. They are magical feats of engineering in the way he has designed their doors, shelves, and drawers, and incorporated symbolism, and function. One is often hard put to locate the door or drawer; it's like hunting for, and finding, the key to a magical kingdom.

Charles B. Cobb's carved and constructed jewelry boxes utilize different woods for color and gouging tool marks for texture. His "teapots" are containers with small drawers or trays that pull out by the knobs. Much sought after by teapot collectors, they are functional as container and sculpture but not as teapots.

Sean Palmer's cantilevered jewelry box has colored inlay circles along with different woods. Stone handles and base are another contrasting element for color and texture.

A surfeit of fabulous forms and surface decorations are mind boggling in the pieces by William McDowell, Chris Martin, Dewey Garrett, Michael J. Brolly, and Jim Kelso. Kelso, who is also a jewelry maker, uses a traditional Japanese metal, called shibuichi, for details.

Urns and reliquary boxes by Michael Creed and Anthony Ulinsky are wonderfully innovative. Creed's limousine shaped piece with a dog image is funky and painted inside and out. It is probably an urn for a dog's ashes. Ulinski, who was born in Indonesia and raised in Africa, Asia, Europe, and the United States brings a wealth of cultural images to his work. His boxes combine traditional joinery, Fijian-inspired carving, paper-and-cane construction techniques adapted from Japanese lantern making, and finishing techniques such as gouging, burning, scarring, and painting.

Norman Sartorius at work on a sculptural spoon. He says, "People look at me rather oddly when I tell them I make non-functional wooden spoons. Non-functional in that you wouldn't use them in the kitchen but functional in that they are objects of beauty. My spoons are sculptures; my sculptures are spoons; not spoons to stir the soup, but spoons to stir the soul." *Photo, Jim Osborn*

Norman Sartorius. **Mutation**. Mexican oak. Burl. 3" high, 9" long, 4" deep. This carving references spoons without being one. It seemed to have an abnormal attachment, hence, a "mutation." Collection, The Renwick Gallery, National Museum of American Art Smithsonian Institution, Washington, D.C. *Photo, Jim Osborn*

What makes an artist turn his skills to reliquaries? Ulinski explained that when he had lost a friend he built a funerary urn. The process led him to a lifelong fascination with ceremonial objects and gave shape to a body of new work dealing with urns and reliquaries, or vessels for sacred personal objects.

Street art is the title given to the many signs that Ghyslain Grenier creates. All signs are carved, hand painted, and decorated with a 23-karat gold leaf finish. The artist stresses that such street art requires the talents of a designer, wood sculptor, sign painter, and gilder. His studio, L'Enseignerie, is the first studio of its kind in Canada to be awarded membership in a prestigious organization of wood artists.

Frank E. Cummings' hair decorations, inspired by African hair combs, are intricately carved and combined with other materials such as stone and glass. For each piece, Cummings has designed a box that is as exquisite as the piece itself. He says, "Many materials that I use and enjoy are not considered sophisticated, and the processes are considered ancient. One of my goals is to bridge ancient philosophies and cultural traditions with contemporary attitudes and classic designs. Another dominant influence in my work is 18th Century Shaker Furniture, not for its austerity, but for its honesty, truth to materials, and the belief that to do a thing well is in itself an act of prayer."

Norman Sartorius. **Pigtail.** African blackwood. This darkest of rosewoods has a buttery texture. The abstracted spoon evolved from the heartwood/sapwood interplay. 8.5" long, 3.5" wide, 1" deep. Collection Malekah Roberts. *Photo, Jim Osborn*

Norman Sartorius. **Free Edge Scoop.** Amboyna burl. Having a jagged edge on the lip of a utensil is counterintuitive. He finds it fun to play with deep-seated assumptions regarding a spoon's characteristics. 9" long, 3" wide, 2" deep. *Photo, Jim Osborn*

Norman Sartorius. **Wholly Holey.** Jarrah burl. Initially, the challenge was to see if he could carve an even bowl from wood so full of holes. Eventually the freedom of the odd bowl led to a very uncharacteristic handle. 7.75" long, 3.25" wide. 2.5" deep. *Collection, John and Robyn Horn. Photo, Jim Osborn*

Giles Gilson. **Early Autumn**. Sculptured feather cabinet on a pedestal. The closed cabinet has three shelves, two drawers, and a black flocked interior. It consists of padauk, lacquered basswood colored tangerine with gold pearl over a white base, lace wood, walnut, cherry, figured maple, ebony, holly, purpleheart, brass, and stainless steel. Bohlen Collection. 28" high, 22" wide, 12" deep. *Photo, Rick Siciliano*

Giles Gilson. **Early Autumn**, open. From the closed view, it's hard to imagine, or detect how the cabinet opens and what the interior looks like. Gilson's imagination and engineering for his cabinets are awesome. *Photo, Rick Siciliano*

Giles Gilson. **Early Autumn**, back view. *Photo, Rick Siciliano*

Charles B. Cobb. **Mary Ellen's Idea**. Earring collection box. Hawaiian koa, African wenge and glass. So named because the client said, "I want a box to hold earrings. You make it; I will love it." 10" high, 15" wide, 15" deep. *Photo, artist*

Sean P. Palmer. **Step Jewelry Box**. Vertical grain white oak and walnut. Inlay is rosewood, walnut, padauk, and purpleheart. Carved blue stone base and handles. 11" high, 10" wide, 4" deep. *Photo, Dona Meilach*

Charles B. Cobb. **Winston's Favorite.** Jewelry box. Hawaiian koa, African wenge, red oak, and paint. The piece was designed around the pattern on the koa drawer fronts. 24" high, 20" wide, 10" deep. *Photo, Sharon Beal*

William McDowell. **Jewelry Box**. Curly maple, Chakte-viga, and African wenge. The orange color of the Mexican Chakte-viga wood contrasts with the dark of the wenge. 5" high, 18" wide, 7" deep. *Photo, Gandino*

Chris Martin. **UFO Box**. Redwood, cottonwood, maple, walnut, and forged steel. 8" high, 10.5" diam. *Photo, artist*

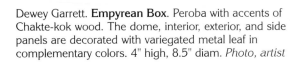

Dewey Garrett. **Empyrean Box**. Peroba with accents of Chakte-kok wood. The dome, interior, exterior, and side panels are decorated with variegated metal leaf in complementary colors. 4" high, 8.5" diam. *Photo, artist*

Michael J. Brolly. **Mary the Baby Sitter**. Ring Holder. Purpleheart and African wenge. 3" high, 6" wide, 7" deep. *Photo, David Haas*

Jim Kelso. **Fern Box**. Ebony, black ash burl, shibuichi, 22K and a 24K gold butterfly. 2.25" high, 2.75" square. *Photo, artist*

Charles B. Cobb. **Teapot Container.** Maple bleached and the handle is dyed black. The top lifts off to reveal a small compartment. 14" high, 10" wide, 16" deep. *Photo, Hap Sakwa*

Charles B. Cobb. **Teapot box**. Walnut, zebra, koa insert, maple drawers, and ball knobs painted copper. The knobs lift out small drawers. 7" high, 7" wide, 5" deep. *Photo, Hap Sakwa*

Charles B. Cobb. **Teapot Box**. Walnut, maple, donut shaped zebrawood, donut handle, and paint ball knob. The knob lifts out a small drawer. 8" high, 8" wide, 5" deep. *Photo, Hap Sakwa*

Michael Creed. **GrrrRover.** Open. The front reveals a drawer and the top lifts to provide another container. *Photo, artist*

Michael Creed. **GrrrRover**. A funerary urn for two, closed. Cherry wood, walnut, dyed bird's eye maple, and paint. 16" high, 27" long, 11" deep. *Photo, artist*

Anthony Ulinski. **Geometric Reliquary**. Closed. Carved and painted hardwoods, bent lamination, traditional joinery, hand-gilded blown glass mirror, and milk paint. 69" high, 14" wide, 9" deep. *Photo, Steve Murray*

Anthony Ulinski. **Geometric Reliquary**. Open. *Photo, Steve Murray*

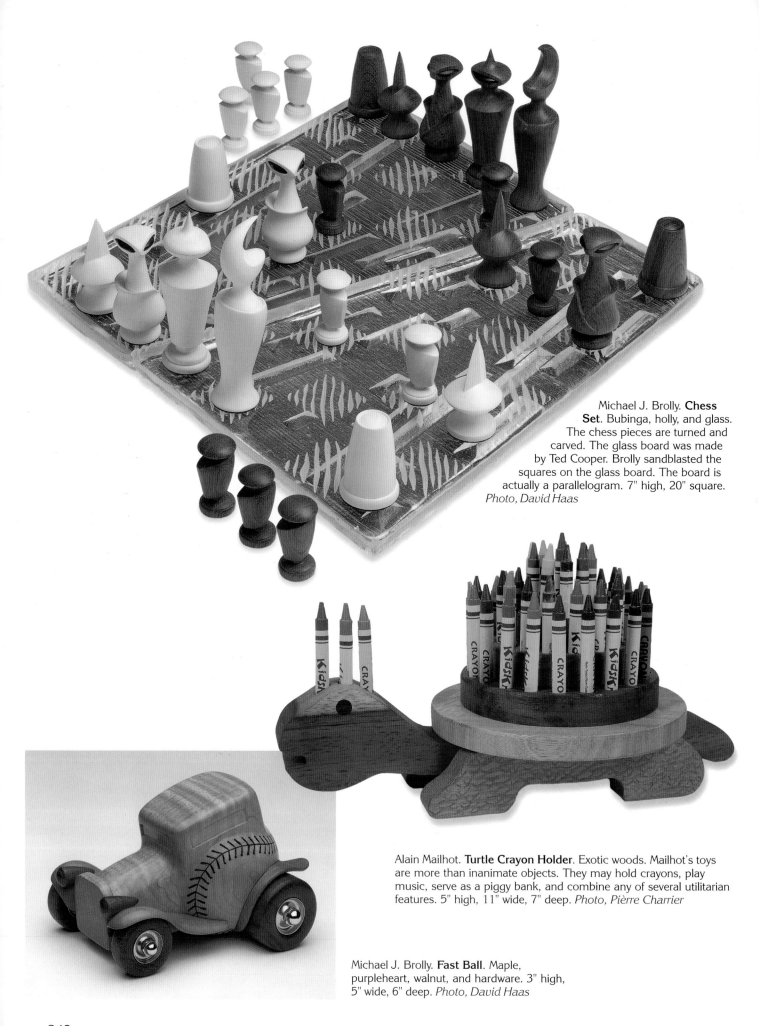

Michael J. Brolly. **Chess Set**. Bubinga, holly, and glass. The chess pieces are turned and carved. The glass board was made by Ted Cooper. Brolly sandblasted the squares on the glass board. The board is actually a parallelogram. 7" high, 20" square. *Photo, David Haas*

Alain Mailhot. **Turtle Crayon Holder**. Exotic woods. Mailhot's toys are more than inanimate objects. They may hold crayons, play music, serve as a piggy bank, and combine any of several utilitarian features. 5" high, 11" wide, 7" deep. *Photo, Pièrre Charrier*

Michael J. Brolly. **Fast Ball**. Maple, purpleheart, walnut, and hardware. 3" high, 5" wide, 6" deep. *Photo, David Haas*

Eliane Kinsley. **Fan**. Spalted maple burl veneer, curly maple covers. Marquetry. Fanning out veneers allows an intimate observation of the variations in character as well as their beauty as they are juxtaposed. 8" radius. *Photo, artist*

Rod W. Layden. **Plane. Baroque No. 3**. Cocobolo and Osage orange. The plane is functional, but really is meant to be a sculptural object. 8" high, 15.5" wide, 3" deep. *Photo, Dona Meilach*

Peter Hromek. **Salt and Pepper Grinders.** Different exotic woods. 14.5" high, 0.9" diam. *Photo, Georg Gottbrath*

Jacques Vesery. **Phlight of Phancy.** Carved cherry with ebony rim and handle, and 23k gold leaf. When smooth surfaces, rough textures, brilliant and deep dark tones, become one, they conjure a world of backyard tea parties, rabbits with watches, and hookah smoking caterpillars. 4" high, 4" diam. Collection, Bruce Raben. *Photo, Robert Diamante*

Michael Hosaluk. **Unusual Fruits**. Arbutus burl, painted wood, copper, and hair. A collection of unusual fruits; "reflective of the many people I know." 12" high, 27" wide, 12" deep. *Photo, artist*

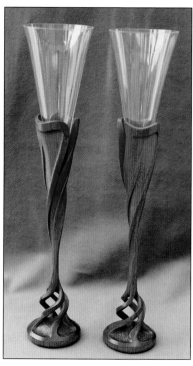

Nikolai Ossipov. **Champagne Goblets.** Mahogany, turned and carved from one piece of wood. Removable glass. 12" high, 2" diam. *del Mano Gallery, Los Angeles, California. Photo, artist*

Nicola Henshaw. **Bird Pots.** Carved lime and gold leaf. Pots vary from 16" to 24" diam. *Photo, Andra Nelki*

David French. **The Fabled Teapots**. Carved wood, oil painted. 8.5" high, 52" wide, 5.75" deep. *Linda Hodges Gallery, Seattle, Washington. Photo, artist*

Chyslain Grenier. **L'Enseignerie**. Street sign. Today, many signs are produced much like cut and paste graphics in a computer. When they are hand carved and customized they become, what the artist calls, "Street Art" and for good reason. *Photo, Artist*

Chyslain Grenier. **L'Enseignerie.** Street sign with hand forged and welded iron bracket. The music clef helps set the theme of the business it represents. *Photo, artist*

Chyslain Grenier. **L'Enseignerie.** Street sign hand carved in deep three dimensions so the camera appears to extend from the background. Both this sign and the Corriveau sign incorporate a negative area so that light and sky become part of the sign's composition. Photographer's portrait by Rosanne Pomerleau. *Photo, artist*

Shirley Miki De Moraes. **Orange Leaves Bracelet**. Wood inlay and silver construction. Paela, bocote, and African wenge, with pearls and sterling silver. 1.25" high, 7.5" long, 0.38" deep. *Photo, Larry Sanders*

Shirley Miki De Moraes. **Botannical Stick Pins.** Wood inlay and silver construction. Yellow heart, paela, red heart, purpleheart, and canary wood, with pearls and sterling silver. Each, 4.5" high, 0.75" wide, 0.38" deep. *Photo, Larry Sanders*

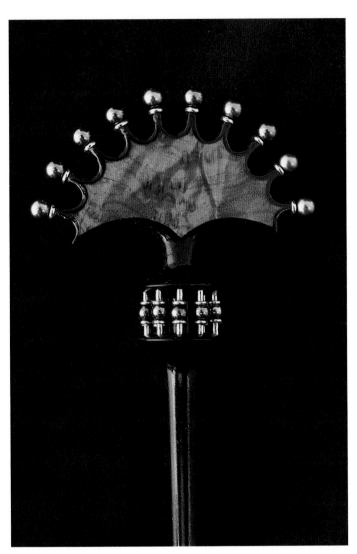

Frank E. Cummings III. **Companion**. Jewelry for the hair, detail. Ebony, chittum burl, with black pearls and 18K gold. 7.75" high, 2.3" wide. *Photo, artist*

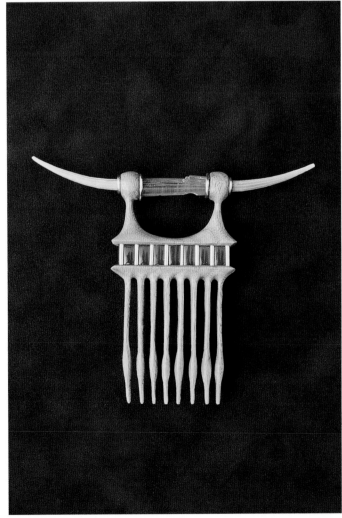

Frank E. Cummings III. **Decorative Hair Comb**. Chakte-vira wood, jeweled crystal, jade, green dentalium shells, and 18k gold. 3.25" high, 4.3" wide. *Photo, Artist*

253

Bibliography

Boase Tony. *Bowl Turning Techniques. Masterclass.* East Sussex, Great Britain: Guild of Master Craftsmen Publications Ltd., 1999.

Hosaluk. Michael. *Scratching the Surface. Art and Content in Contemporary Wood.* Guild. 2002.

Ketchum, William C. Jr., Nancy Akre, Editor. *Boxes.* NewYork, New York: Cooper-Hewitt Museum; the Smithsonian Institution, 1982.

Leistikow, Klaus Ulrich. *The Woodbook.* Los Angeles, California: Taschen America Ltd, 2002.

Lincoln, William A. *World Woods In Color.* New York, New York: Macmillan Publishing Co., 1986.

Lydgate, Tony and Po Shun Leong. *Art Boxes.* New York, New York: Sterling Publishing Co., 1998.

Olson, Garry and Peter Toaig. *One tree.* Columbus, Ohio: Merrell Publishers, 2001.

Pierce, Kerry. *The Custom Furniture Sourcebook: A Guide to 125 Craftsmen.* New York, New York: Sterling Publishing Co., 2001.

Pilot Productions; Introduction by John Makepeace. *The Art of Making Furniture.* New York, New York: Sterling Publishing Co., 1981.

Plotnik, Arthur. *The Urban Tree Book.* Times Books, 2000.

Raffan, Richard. *Turning Wood.* Newton, Connecticut: Taunton Press, 2001.

Simpson, Chris. *The Essential Guide to Woodwork.* San Diego, California: Thunder Bay Press. (British Imprint), 2002.

Wood Turning Center & Yale University. *Wood Turning in North America Since 1930.* Philadelphia, Pennsylvania: 2001.

Resources

A search for woodworking books on the Internet will reveal many titles dealing with one or more disciplines such as Furniture, Turning, Tables, etc. Some dealers specialize in woodworking books.

Internet. Search for:

1. Any type of wood and it will lead you to the sources that sell it, discuss it, and link you to a variety of other resources. For example, look up lacewood, or padouk, or purpleheart.
2. Wood working
3. Wood organizations
4. Wood associations
5. Wood turners
6. Names of specific artists
7. Exotic woods
8. Magazines, wood
9. Books about wood turning

Also:

Collectors of Wood Art
Forest Products Laboratory
Guild.com
International Sculpture Society
International Wood Collectors Society
Righteous Woods
American Association of Woodturners
Furniture Society
Wood Turning Center

Index

A
Allergies, 19
Altug, Mehmet Sahin, 100, 101
B
Barrish, Jerry Ross, 186, 194
Bauermeister, Michael, 138, 163
Benches, 46-53
Bencomo, Derek, 175, 176
Bennett, Garry Knox, 42, 46, 50, 81, 83, 115
Benson, Jonathan, 23, 29, 118
Betts, James, 28
Boomer, John, 236
Brolly, Michael J., 53, 68, 109, 119, 196, 197, 239, 245, 248
Buck, John, 184-186
Burchard, Christian, 159
Burls, 11, 13, 132, 175-183
C
Cabinets, 84-107
Carlin, David, 231, 232
Carving, surface, 152-158
Castle, Wendell, 31, 94
Chappelow, William V., 15, 238
Christensen, Kip, 143, 173
Christiansen, James, 141
Clocks, 108-114
Cobb Charles B., 28, 29, 37, 39, 65, 98, 121-124, 239, 243, 246, Front Cover
Color, 11, 18, 164-174
Connover-Loar, Kim, 219
Cooper, Ted, 248
Couradin, Jean- Christophe, 206
Courtney, Stephen, 23, 29, 30, 71, 73, 81
Creed, Michael, 39, 40, 67, 72, 82, 239, 247
Cummings III, Frank E., 130, 144, 145, 240,253
Curing a log, 12
D
Davis, Derek Secor, 31, 39, 41, 51, 72, 76, 77, 116, Front Cover
DeGirolamo, John E., 32, 69,
Desks, 70-83
DiNovi, Victor, 31, 49, 59, 118, 121, 123
Drying, 12, 13
Dunbrack, Rick, 109, 112, 113

E
Elliott, Dennis, 18, 180, 204, 233
Ellsworth, David, 131, 219
Elvig, Glenn, 204, 233
F
Figure in wood, 10
Fleming, Pat, 165, 166, 173
Fleming, Ron, 131, 152, 154, 156, 157, 164-166
Foster, Clay, 153, 171
Foster, Michael R., 223
Frank, Elizabeth, 185, 192
French, David, 250
Furniture, 20-125
G
Garrett, Dewey, 171, 203, 239, 244
Gerton, Ron, 175, 177, 178
Gilson, Giles, 186, 198, 199, 239, 242
Gleasner, Stephen, 136, 137
Glues, 18
Grain, 10
Grenier, Chyslain, 240, 251
Groth, David, 8, 188-191
Guillerm, Philippe, 199
H
Hardwoods, 10
Hart, Edward, 186-195
Heitzman, Roger, 72, 75, 86-89, 234, Back cover
Henshaw, Nicola, 17, 39, 40, 44-46, 66, 234, 235, 250
Hibbert, Louise, 162
Hill, Matthew, 162
Holzapfel, David, 26, 27
Holzapfel, Michelle, 152, 186, 211-213, 226, 228-230, Back cover
Hooper, Richard, 186, 205, 206
Horn, Robyn, 186, 205, 222, 234
Hosaluk, Michael, 39, 43, 67, 250, Back cover
Hromek, Peter, 144, 146, 160, 249
Hunter, William, 130, 144, 148, 149, 170, 207, 208
I
Inskeep, Kate, 116
Internet, 19
Ireland, Michael, 39, 84, 85, 99
Isham, Tex, 200